Make Your Own Way: An Individual's Guide to Fulfillment

MATT DELLAERO

Copyright © 2024 Matt Dellaero

All rights reserved.

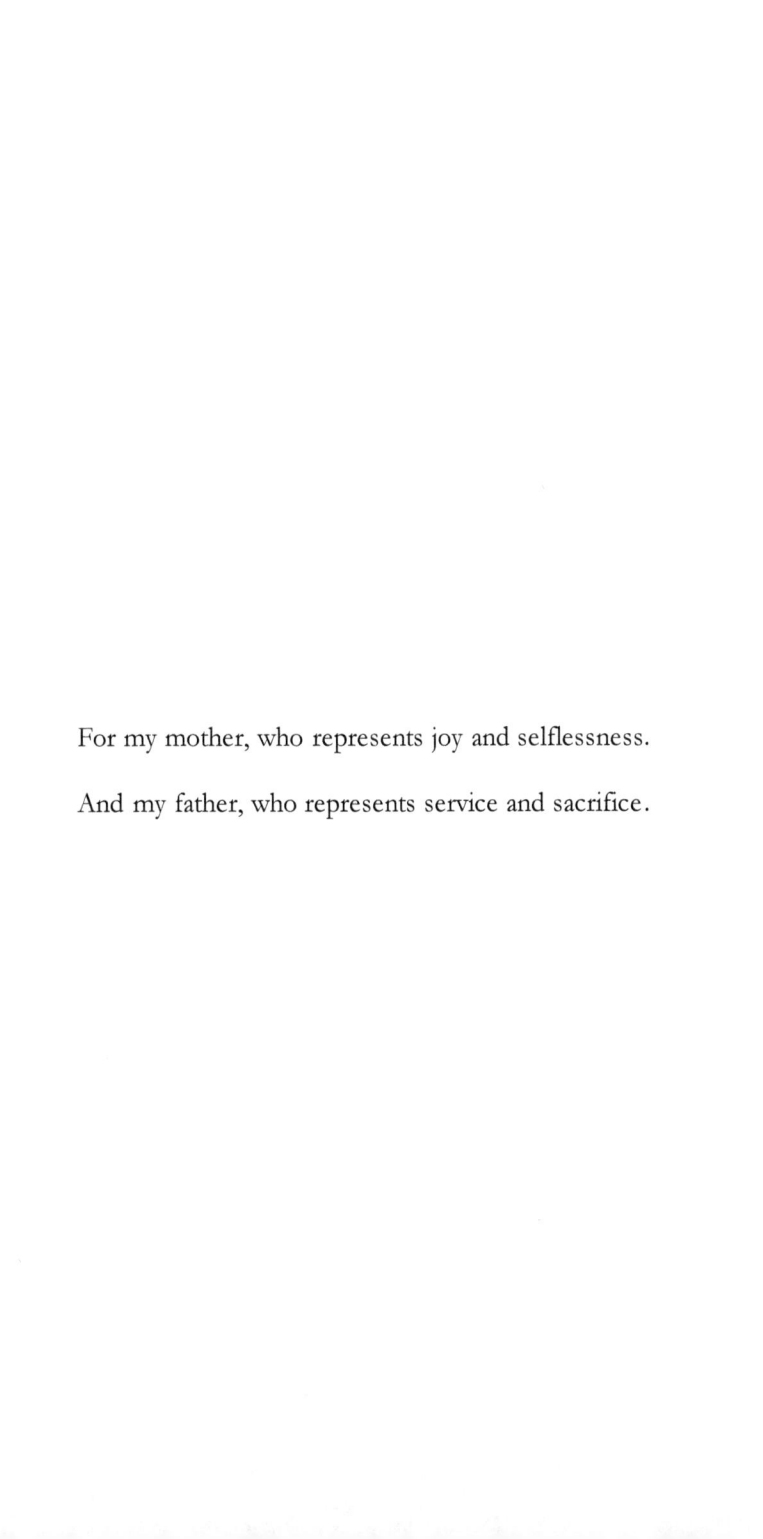

For my mother, who represents joy and selflessness.

And my father, who represents service and sacrifice.

CONTENTS

	Preface	ix

Health:

1	Animal First, Human Second	1
2	Your First Relationship	8
3	Reactionary	13
4	Master of Adaptation	17

Mental:

5	The Illusion of Control	21
6	Overcoming	26
7	Training Your Guard Dog	32
8	The Observer	38

Wealth:

9	"Enough"	44
10	Monthly Magic	48
11	Living Guilt-Free	53

Relationships:

12	Know Yourself in Others	59
13	The Importance of Unconditionality	63
14	Tend to Your Roots	67

Work & Hobbies:

	15	One in Eight Billion	72
	16	Exercise Your Mind	76
	17	The Art of Spending Time	80

Meaning Making:

	18	*Tetsugaku*	87
	19	Using "Temporary" to Your Advantage	92
	20	Too Soft, Too Hard; Just Right	97
	21	The Mind Is a Mirror	101
	22	When Hedonism Reigns	106
	23	Something Bigger, Something More	111

Selflessness:

	24	Lost at the Mountaintop	115
	25	The Caring Creature	119
	26	How to Feed Your Ego (the Right Way)	123
	27	Honor	127

Death:

	28	Relax, You've Done This Before	131
	29	Borrowed Time	135
	30	The Opposite of Lonely	139

		Acknowledgements	143

"If your ship doesn't come in, swim out to it!"

– Jonathan Winters

PREFACE

I fear a world in which people live without hope, stuck in loneliness, failing to make the most of their lives due to a lack of self-belief—now is not the first time that humans find themselves in this position. This state of despondency in the world seems to ebb and flow throughout history, depending on how much meaning and connection can be found in our lives, and our ability to experience life fully.

Life will never run out of problems to solve, but happiness and meaning are achievable in the time that we have here. My goal is to arm people with the necessary tools to feel capable, connected, and excited about life.

The amount of information and choice that exists in our world can feel overwhelming, but that is exactly where the opportunity exists.

This book is for anyone interested in taking wisdom from multiple fields and applying it to their own life, or anyone wishing to maximize their potential. The application of the wisdom from this book would result in two things:

1. Developing a lifestyle that allows you to experience satisfaction and fulfillment on a daily basis throughout your journey.
2. Making a positive impact on others, which would create a ripple effect that would improve the world.

Ultimately this book is for anyone looking to improve

their life in any area, from meeting basic needs to finding a deeper purpose.

The inspiration for this book draws on three main ideas:

1. The Lost Generation: A demographic of people in a post-war era who, after witnessing and experiencing mass trauma, were described as directionless.
2. Maslow's Hierarchy of Needs: A psychologist's theory on human needs.
3. Friedrich Nietzsche's Übermensch: The concept of a human who embodies these attributes – self-determination, creativity, becoming, overcoming, discontent, flexibility, self-mastery, self-confidence, cheerfulness, and courage.

Throughout this book we will revisit the theory which states that you must first understand your nature before you can go on to do great things in your life. Imagine that we are starting with the foundation as we arrange your life like building blocks, one section at a time. What is the use of a good foundation? Solid ground that will serve you through the many changes and challenges of life. This applies to your physical, psychological, and even financial habits. Are you too tight or too loose? Doing too much or too little in these areas? Later, we will explore the importance of defining and then doing "enough" in any area of your life. Too much can border on the obsessive, while too little becomes a bit underachieving. Balance is the goal because balance is sustainable.

The other main idea is that you can start from wherever you are now and take full responsibility for your life.

That willingness costs nothing, but opens the door to each new opportunity. It's hard to be a social animal. There is overwhelming influence that pulls you in every direction and makes it unclear what you should do, or who you should be. This book invites you to reject that influence and instead make your own way.

Rather than attempting to explain "what" is important in life, which you have probably already heard, this book is meant to highlight the "why" and "how." Why should you care about your body, mind, relationships, and spirituality? What role do these play in living a satisfying life? How can you approach difficult and nuanced topics such as mental health? And finally, how do you think about death?

By the end of this book, you will feel a new sense of personal security, agency, and urgency. You will know yourself better based on what resonates with you. You will think more clearly in your day-to-day, and most importantly, you will feel confident in your ability to spend your energy wisely.

This book should be read with a sense of curiosity. The answers you find in yourself are more valuable than what anyone else can give you. Hopefully, as you read, you will find inspiration to create new ideas on your own. Your calling is to create the best version of yourself by understanding your unique strengths and weaknesses. With that being said, we begin with the foundation: your animal and human nature.

Section I: Foundational Needs

1. ANIMAL FIRST, HUMAN SECOND

*"It is human nature to think wisely
and act in an absurd fashion."*

– Anatole France

Ask yourself with complete honesty: are you an animal, a human, or both?

Imagine that when you wake up: a lizard, a monkey, and a sophisticated human all reach for the steering wheel in the control center of your mind. One—driven by survival, demanding that you need water, food, coffee, then the bathroom. The next—basic thoughts and feelings: dread, apprehension, as well as some excitement. And finally at the highest level— a clear set of goals and intentions for the day. Can you successfully satisfy all three in a given day while also taking care of your family, responsibilities, and unexpected challenges? No wonder life seems overwhelming at times.

Here, the lizard and the monkey are just metaphors to explain the complex inner workings that drive us each day. And it can become even more complicated. A significant experience that overstimulates certain parts of your mind can skew your internal balance to the point where you don't even feel like "you" are in the driver's seat anymore. Obviously, the goal is for everything to communicate and stay in harmony, but it's going to take some work and practice; it's okay to need practice.

Your body and mind are your two greatest resources, and learning how to manage both effectively will lead to a great deal of life satisfaction. Thankfully, the body and mind have unbelievable powers of self-repair and regulation. Getting there, and giving yourself what you need to have a smooth running system, is typically the challenge. Part of it is "letting go of control," sure, but another part of it is having a good sense of control over what actually deserves attention. Understanding your core needs will allow you to become more physically and psychologically whole.

First, let's talk about when the "lizard brain" has too much control. This can be difficult or painful, but it is important to address. Anyone with a traumatic or near-death experience may be able to relate to the feelings of hypervigilance—living in survival mode. Fear in the form of worst-case scenario, all-or-nothing "what if" questioning. Thoughts and behaviors that feel automatic and outside of your control. And in a sense, they are. Sometimes the best you can do is to simply remain aware of these impulses so that they do not fully control you. Trying to act on them or change them directly is seemingly not very effective but this part of our system is still important. So, you can't get rid of it entirely. After all, you have to eat, you have to sleep, and you have to use the bathroom. In general, you want to have that part of your brain that helps you survive, right?

Without directly controlling this system, you might be amazed how much influence you have over it through repeated exposure. The theme of control versus influence will remain relevant throughout this book since influence is where you need to put your focus and effort.

Let's say you are afraid of driving, flying, darkness, public speaking, or isolation. The object of your fear is less important than what is really going on when you feel controlled by that survival instinct which is very real. The fear is imagined— if you're reading this right now then you're very safe— but the instinct and reaction are real. To rewire this part, maybe an overreaction to a specific fear, is going to take some courage.

People will walk through life trying many things to get rid of that survival instinct when it is really just trying to do its job. Addiction is one of the most common patterns, although these patterns vary and avoiding them usually involves unhealthy activities. When you realize this, it is a lot harder to judge someone for their addictions and impulses. They probably experienced something agonizing or hard to understand, and walked away from it with less of an understanding of themselves. So, here comes the bit about courage:

It starts with surrender.

It's incredibly hard. It feels like giving up control while

allowing yourself to go *through* the pain and uncertainty. It's choosing to face, feel, and accept what you've been avoiding. The lizard brain does not want you to get in that car, or the plane, or to find yourself alone. But again, if you are reading this book right now, you're surviving just fine and your systems are up and running. Our goal is to start from where you are now and create a better future. For that to happen, it starts with surrendering so that the lizard brain realizes something important: you're not going to die.

You are going to die, of course, just not because you feel so, even when everything around you is fine. If you repeat that action of surrender, something amazing happens. The lizard brain begins to self-regulate and work as designed. And that, in and of itself, is a great reward. Future sections will examine the lizard brain and how it relates to control and anxiety but for now, we've established the basic idea of surrendering in the face of an imagined threat (or the echo of one that was once very real in the case of trauma).

Let's say that, with some practice, you move past the survival part of life. That alone deserves celebrating and you might find yourself back there at some point, but at least you can move past it with practice and exposure. Next, we shift our attention to what is frequently referred to as "the monkey mind."

This may very well be the most annoying part of human psychology. Sure, the lizard brain can be tough to tame, but at least, it's directly focused on helping you survive. That seems important. The monkey, for whatever reason, is more intent on pulling you in different directions, presenting all manner of random thoughts and ideas that make it difficult to focus. It jumps from one thing to the next and rarely feels satisfied. Compared to the lizard brain which needs the feeling of safety and surrender, the monkey mind requires something different: some discipline and self-control.

It doesn't make sense to live all the time with feelings of restlessness, insecurity, and distraction. But again, you do need this part of your brain. Emotions and the ability to complete some complex tasks without using too much energy or thought are aided by the same part of your brain that says "what about this?" and "have you thought about this?" and "did you forget about that?" Understanding how to define "enough" for yourself, in any area of your life will go a long way in helping the monkey mind feel satisfied— finding that balance of doing what needs to be done while reaching a point of satisfaction, self-assurance and peace of mind. Believe it or not, the monkey wants you to rest, too; it's just not always sure about how to get there.

In the chapter titled, "The Observer," we'll dive into the role that you, the reader, play in regulating the monkey mind. But for now, it's helpful to understand that you don't want to rid yourself of these thoughts. You just don't want to get tangled up in them, either. When you master your relationship with this part of your mind, your thoughts and emotions can flow without struggle. Healthy emotional regulation happens here, in your ability to recognize your thoughts and feelings. The monkey mind can be helpful in providing input about your world, and if you learn how to be fully present, the great reward is a fine-tuned intuition.

Now, getting back to the original question: are you an

animal, a human, or both? Whether your goal is to get out of survival mode, to stop overthinking, or to experience life more fully, it begins with understanding your nature.

In a sense, you are an animal first, and then, a human. Denying or suppressing that nature leaves you with less control. When you focus only on our society and world built out of human ideas, you may bypass your core needs, but the primal, natural and emotional aspects of your being are incredibly valuable. When they are out of sync, panic, dread, anxiety, depression, overthinking, paranoia and confusion become present and you might feel the need to run or hide from yourself. But when survival needs are met and emotions are regulated, you leave room to become something truly special: the person who you *really* are.

Throughout this book, we will explore what it means to be a healthy human. You could go as far as to say that much of the struggle and pain in this world is created out of completely dysregulated "lizard brains" and "monkey minds." With that understanding, it is a lot easier to find sympathy for your fellow humans who probably want the same things as you.

When things are working as they should, however, the body and mind function in a divine symphony. You can flow through tasks with ease, generate new ideas with flexible and dynamic thinking, and find peace in every day. You will feel the alignment you have created within yourself, which will always make life worth living. While they can be difficult to manage, the animal parts of our nature lend us the ability to enjoy so much: food, sex, exercise, sleep, and more.

Continuing that theme is going to help if you have a mastery over your very first relationship in life– the one that you came into this world with, the contract you maintain with your body.

2. YOUR FIRST RELATIONSHIP

"The groundwork for all happiness is health."

– Leigh Hunt

Among the many joys and pains that come with being human, the body can seem like a boon or a limitation to how you live your life. When your body feels great, there's nothing like it. But when something is wrong and you're in pain, everything else around you ceases to matter. Good health is truly a gift and fortunately, your body's nature is to be fairly resilient. While not perfect, the body has methods of compensating and adapting... with a bit of help.

Listening is a crucial skill in life. When you don't listen, you might feel out of touch in your relationships and that includes the relationship you have with your own body. Good listening requires patience, focusing and refocusing attention, curiosity and presence. These same skills apply to how you listen to your body, and here's why:

The nervous system extends far beyond your thoughts and the activity in your mind. You can connect deeply with your body; this is the *feeling* of being "grounded."

When people talk about being grounded, the physical aspect of that is getting out of your head and into your body. It may seem like a small thing but it can save you. Having an awareness of your body is more than just knowing it is there. The body is surprisingly effective at communicating its needs at any given time, but again, you have to practice your ability to listen.

Try it now– get out of your head and into your body. Is it comfortable and pleasing or is it a bit unnerving? If this feels strange, you might realize that you spend most of your time in your head and not enough time in your body. That's fine and common. But the truth is that you aren't alone when you're living with this body.

You co-exist in your own body with beneficial bacteria, fungi, viruses and more. The microbes in your body help you survive as they maintain an intimate relationship with your nervous system, among other processes. So, as it stands, you really aren't just living and caring for yourself alone; you're supporting an entire ecosystem!

And if that weren't enough, how you treat your health will undoubtedly have an impact on your surrounding environment as well as your children's health and well-being.

It's your body, so how much you care about that is entirely up to you. But you have this relationship with your body, a relationship with nature, and relationships with other humans in your world. So, you can start to see how your own health and well-being probably affects much more than just you alone. For that reason, it can be deemed a responsibility. It is fairly common for people to neglect their body in the same way that people neglect their mind as well as their relationships. This only leads to more dysfunction in our world. What initially seems like a personal decision ends up having unintended consequences, for ourselves and often for others, too.

By this point, we've highlighted the importance of caring for your body and the animal parts of your nature, but there is another important observation here. In this mutual relationship, the body can also help the mind.

We know many things that help the body to feel better: quality food, sunlight, exercise, rest, and a good laugh. But what ability do you have to use the body as a tool to support your mind? Maybe you can relate to this experience:

You encounter a stressful thought or a difficult feeling. You begin to think and think, and as you think it through, you seem to be going in circles (probably because you weren't calm when you started off in the first place). Before you know it, your head is spinning and you're worse off than where you began, now feeling overwhelmed and unable to think clearly. Thinking is clearly not calming you down nor is it solving the initial problem or worry… It is time to surrender again, then rescue yourself with some help from the body.

Breath control is stress control.

Grab control of your breath and start with a big one. Usually, increasing activity in your mind is not the best way to calm down. Now, take another breath. Things are starting to feel better. Breathe again with a long exhale. Time is slowing down. One more breath; each one gets easier. Finally, another deep breath and long exhale. The mind has quieted and you are back to that feeling of calm.

Simple, but it's necessary. Your body can tell your mind that you are safe, which it sometimes needs to hear. This is a powerful function of the relationship between body and mind. Think of breathing as a method to offload stress. Breathe your way through stress and understand that you may have to keep going until the stressor has passed.

Usually, you are just a deep breath or a good meal away from feeling better. Understand that this is part of listening to your body. Your stomach is brilliant— stress is intertwined with hunger in a way that allows your body to let you know what you need. Life is busy and it's normal to develop poor habits that ignore these basic inputs from your body, instead of listening to them. But it's rewarding when your body feels safe and comfortable.

Trauma survivors and those who deal with high levels of stress will often struggle to feel safe in their body—a sure sign of a damaged relationship between body and mind. They might dissociate or feel "out of body." This requires a high degree of patience and self-compassion to repair that delicate relationship. Taking time to feel your inner body awareness, connecting to the breath, and listening to your body's needs can all go a long way towards getting back on track.

Your body will fight hard to keep you alive. All you have to do is move it, feed it, and rest it.

Help your body and it will help you. You don't have to be perfect— a little bit of care goes a long way— but this body is your home and it can make your life a lot easier or harder depending on how you treat it. A clear mind and a healthy body allow you to function at the highest level as a human and that is really what this book is about.

3. REACTIONARY

"I never worry about action, but only about inaction."

– Winston S. Churchill

Life is short and you shouldn't take it too seriously, though at the same time, we often underestimate the value and impact of our efforts. The main issue lies with the failure to recognize your influence (not control— more on this later) over future outcomes, as well as the consequences of not taking action. Again, our decisions affect us and others; it's not just you alone. Trying to absolve yourself of any personal responsibility only works for temporary relief. As is the case with anything in life, it's easy to take good health for granted but hard to get it back once it's gone, and good decisions tend to compound as much as bad ones.

Humans are generally not *good* at worrying— we tend to worry about the wrong things with no real ability to see the future. People who worry about money often have had a negative experience with it in the past. The same is true for relationships, work, and health. What you care about is influenced by positive or, more likely, negative past experiences. It's the past projected forward. Can you recognize any ongoing patterns like this in your life right now?

Maybe you worry about money because you felt like you never had enough growing up, but all the while, you neglect the health of your body. You manage to save up enough money, only to find out that your health is going to severely limit your ability to travel and enjoy life. Or you follow a similar story, but with your mental health. You once lost your job and now job security is a major focus in your life. That's fine, but then you become a workaholic and begin to neglect your mental well-being. Maybe you focus on your health and finances, but then your relationships suffer.

What you *should* be worried about is often the thing you are not currently worried about. The object of your concern after a negative experience is usually long gone and, because you worried about it, is probably going to be fine in the future. There is a Japanese proverb, *"Ichibyou sokusai"*, which translates to "one illness, good health." Those who have experienced the consequences of poor health may take better care of themselves to live better and longer compared to someone who takes their good health for granted. There is no need to wait for a bad experience before improving how you care for your body.

The main difference between health and other common worries, such as work, relationships, and money, is that many of these issues can be fixed or reversed. Good health, on the other hand, is a continuous long game. Without the foundation of good physical health, it's going to be far more difficult to enjoy the other things that you worry about. And even if your main concern is money, for example, wouldn't you want to avoid the tremendous costs associated with healthcare?

Now, you can get lucky. And thankfully many health conditions can be reversed or managed. But the ones that can't? The sad truth is that many health issues could simply be avoided if we chose to care before it was too late. Think of good health as a resource that can be managed and maintained.

The advice to exercise and eat right doesn't really mean anything until you value the good health you have now, or when you're working to fix the poor health you find yourself in later. Try to imagine that somewhere down the line, you find out that you have a major illness or disease. How would you react to that news?

Some will say, "That's a problem for the future." There's no denying that; it's just that, it's your future. You will have to feel it and face it when it affects your life, your children's lives, your friends', or the life of anyone else who may have to bear the burden of your care. Too often, we fail to project the consequences of our decisions and then it's too late.

But let's step back into the present. The point of this book is not to make you fear the future, but to help you understand your responsibility and agency towards it. Actions now will invariably change future outcomes and that gives you a great deal of power today. And fortunately, you don't have to do everything right. You only have to do "enough." Take care of your body so that your health can become an afterthought or an assumption which allows you to pursue what really makes you human.

Listen to your body, eat natural foods and you'll feel better. Rest and move your body, trust your intuition and let nature take care of the rest.

Good decisions keep your options open in life. Just as there are negative consequences to poor decision making, healthy decisions lead to exciting results which compound over time.

4. MASTER OF ADAPTATION

*"Your life does not get better by chance,
it gets better by change."*

– Jim Rohn

The cheetah runs at the speed of a car in order to catch its prey. The walrus carries blubber to keep warm and survive in the absence of a food source. The butterfly develops camouflage to blend in with its environment and hide from predators.

These are just a few examples of how living beings adapt to their environment, but for most of these creatures, they adapt unknowingly, simply doing what they need to do to survive. They exist in accordance with nature. Humans are no exception to this rule.

The only difference is that humans have the unique

privilege to develop certain adaptations by choice. You can make choices around how you react to your environment, and as a result of those choices, you adapt. You can train your strength, speed, flexibility, resilience, willpower, and even your attention. Anxiety and depression are patterns that you don't want to stay stuck in, but they are adaptive nonetheless. You learn anxiety as a result of a negative experience that occurred in the past or a perceived concern about the future. You create resilience by focusing on how you respond to stressors and challenges. The lists of physical and mental adaptations available are nearly infinite and can range from powerful and helpful to purely maladaptive.

The idea here is that you can generally choose, or life will choose for you.

That theme will continue as you build your foundation, both in the physical and mental space. You do not determine your circumstances in life, so the majority of your life is instead shaped by how you react to and interact with your environment—action, reaction, then the resulting adaptation. And since you are reading this book, you have the power of choice to begin exerting influence on yourself and the world around you. That starts with your body and mind.

So, what would you choose?

Strength developed by resistance.
Endurance developed by distance.
Speed developed by training.
Flexibility developed by stretching.
Resilience developed by repetition.
Attention developed by focus.

You have all the power to change. Adaptations are real-life superpowers and it's up to you to decide how many you want to leave on the table. Any of these are accessible and each one that you choose will add a new element to your being. As you go out into the world and take action, your mind will change, too. Don't doubt your ability to develop superpowers. No one is a master in the beginning and skill is acquired through practice. Use the analogy of a rusty wheel: at first, establishing new habits around diet and exercise seem frustrating and difficult to maintain. With repetition and practice, however, they become second nature and they are built into your life as a new expectation—you will come to look forward to these changes and how they make your body feel. The change is created through a bit of discipline, but it gets consistently easier over time as the wheel keeps spinning.

Stress is not something to be avoided; it must be pursued and faced if you want the growth that is just on the other side.

When you exercise, the body changes in response to stress. When you exercise regularly, the body continues to adapt and those changes become lasting. Beyond the aesthetic appeal of maintaining a healthy body lies the more valuable internal changes that carry an array of benefits: improved mood, sleep, immune function, energy, ability to carry out daily tasks and more. Everything, down to the cellular level, becomes healthier and stronger. If it helps, think of it as the best method to put more time back on the clock of your life. The outcomes of good health and longer life are a byproduct of your willingness to apply effort.

If you take care of your physical and mental well-being first, it suddenly becomes a lot easier to navigate the rest of life's challenges because you've given yourself the tools to handle them. Who doesn't want to face life with fewer anxieties about their own capability?

With a foundation of good physical health in place, it only makes sense to continue the journey into your greatest resource: the mind.

5. THE ILLUSION OF CONTROL

*"I can control my destiny, but not my fate.
Destiny means there are opportunities to turn right or left,
but fate is a one-way street."*

– Paul Coelho

Try to think of a time when you felt powerless or helpless in a given situation. You wished for a different outcome, but despite how you felt, things didn't seem to go your way (or maybe things didn't work out for a person you love), and it all falls apart. You spend time in your head, reviewing the situation in hopes that you can better understand what went wrong or maybe to figure out how you can still somehow change the outcome if it's not too late. Things go wrong, anyway, despite our best efforts. Everyone has been there and it's painful.

This control gap you feel can be quite defeating, if that is the area you choose to focus. The more you focus on what is out of your control, the more helpless you might feel. It's enough to give up before even trying in the first place and there is an overwhelming amount of information about what is out there and what is possibly out of your control.

The truth is that focusing only on results and outcomes will inevitably lead to disappointment and fatigue, mainly because you can expect certain outcomes, but not control them. This is the illusion of control.

You can, however, learn to maximize your ability to influence events and feel proud of your efforts in that process. The more you focus on your process and influence, the more your influence grows. As your influence grows, you become more and more empowered to take action. And in that cycle, you influence events and outcomes even more as you continue to take action. Despite the fact that you do not have complete control, you do have a great deal of influence over your health, well-being, and more. You are probably far more capable than you realize; the failure to recognize the full extent of your influence in life is often due to self-defeating patterns of thinking, which cause us to miss potential opportunities.

Focus only on your process in anything—health, wealth, work—and let the results come on their own like setting up dominoes, then letting them fall.

Internalizing the chaos and unpredictability of the world will sap your energy, which could be used instead to improve your life or the lives of others around you. When you choose to become centered, and work from where you are now, your influence can only grow. Your process becomes more consistent and you will find yourself becoming more capable and effective over time.

Then, as you work on yourself and your process, you will begin to realize something important:

The results of external events can never deliver your happiness, because your happiness does not belong to these events; it belongs to you. Your happiness is uniquely defined by you. It's great when things go your way and you can appreciate this in the moment, but you also know that life is a game of highs and lows. Attributing happiness and success only to events outside of your control is ultimately self-defeating. If you judge yourself based on what happens to you, then life isn't going to make very much sense. Place your emphasis on maximizing the influence you have and judging yourself based on your process, which can be repeated, rather than outcomes which may be unpredictable. You are giving yourself the physical and mental foundation to face the unknown.

Understanding control versus influence is key because it is the distinction between being quite capable versus feeling helpless.

While you may not be able to control the events of life, there is something deeply satisfying about having control over ourselves and our reactions to those events. There is a peace of mind that comes from knowing there is nothing you could or should be doing differently.

Now, with all of that being said, it is still perfectly normal to worry. In the first chapter, we took a brief look at the "monkey mind" and the way it jumps from one thought to the next. In the upcoming chapters, we will explore resilience, managing anxiety and worry, and ultimately how to observe and regulate the mind. But before we can do that, it's necessary to highlight the benefits of letting go of control. Letting go of control is a skill after all, especially after a negative experience. The more you let go of control, the more you realize that you never had it in the first place.

By that same logic, the best reason not to worry is that it won't change anything in reality—simple as that. It does take discipline and it isn't easy. Effective thinking and planning are different from worry, and you can aim to recognize the difference; nothing bad will happen if you dismiss unhelpful thinking. So let's revisit that idea one last time.

Experiencing the control gap includes worry, fear of the uncertain, feeling inadequate or helpless.

Focus on your influence includes effective thinking and planning, taking action, and feeling capable.

Remember when we focused on the idea of surrender in the first chapter? It directly applies here. In this context, surrender does not mean giving up or giving in. It's specifically about letting go of the illusion of control. Logically, it's the only thing that makes sense. Emotionally, it takes a great deal of courage because vulnerability requires bravery, not certainty. You are committed to not knowing the outcome. When you surrender control, you trust yourself completely to handle the uncertainty of the future and that will only increase your feelings of capability. That is how you give yourself personal power and influence.

And in another sense, uncertainty can be a blessing. It confirms that your worries about the future aren't accurate because you do not and cannot know the future. So, regardless of whether you expect good or bad things to happen in the future, it serves you well to let go of control either way.

The final piece that goes hand-in-hand with surrendering control is an understanding that life can be met with an attitude of acceptance. Acceptance will serve you well by allowing you to avoid a lot of unnecessary suffering. Again, just as it was the case with surrender, practicing acceptance does not mean rolling over and giving up. In many cases, especially with negative outcomes, it does not even mean endorsement or approval. The opposite is true. Acceptance is a commitment to what is true and real under the present circumstances, and it gives way for action without anything holding you back.

When you organize each idea, thought, or worry into the appropriate bucket—inside or outside of your control—a clear picture of what you are able to influence and overcome develops. Anyone that begins with self-doubt can move to a place of self-belief through action.

6. OVERCOMING

"You may encounter many defeats but you must not be defeated."

– Maya Angelou

Often attributed to Buddhism is the belief that our life and existence are suffering due to our attachments. Well, that's not particularly motivating, nor is it entirely fair or accurate to the human story. There is suffering in life, but if that encapsulated our entire existence, then nothing would move forward. Our shared humanity is built on progress and evolution, and if not for our attachments, we would not likely see much reason to put forth effort each day. Besides, it takes a great deal of vulnerability to form attachments, knowing that they are temporary. You are here to overcome, not suffer.

In the previous chapter, we identified the control gap.

If we apply that in the sense of overcoming, a mastery of life might look something like: putting maximum effort into the things you care about and control, combined with a willingness to completely let go of everything else. It takes effort, and there is real friction in the process of doing this, but it's also the only logical thing to do. And it's an ongoing practice.

The more information available, the more difficult it becomes to take action because of a higher perception of potential risk. On your journey, you should expect to encounter things outside of your control that are painful or difficult to understand. You can choose to spend time contemplating these external events or you can peacefully let them go. By letting go, you conserve energy for everything else that is still in your control.

As you work to hone your focus and attention with this practice, you can begin to take responsibility for your life.

Responsibility does not mean that you have to do everything alone. What it means is that, through your own efforts and with help from others, you are taking ownership with a willing attitude to change and grow. *That* is the central thesis of this book: you have ownership of your life as well as the ability to improve and enjoy it, not based on "what" you think, but rather by "how" you think and approach life. Thus far, you have two key traits which you can use to face life:

- A healthy physical foundation
- An attitude of acceptance

And now, you combine these traits with the desire to

overcome. Taking responsibility for your life is not easy, but it is the first step towards living the life that you want. A willingness to face and overcome new challenges will only further your desire to see how far you can go. But you have to start small.

Let's say you wake up and you are met with any mixture of dread or apprehension— feelings of unease and uncertainty about what the day may bring. Let these feelings melt away on their own. Don't feel the need to force them away or avoid them. Tap into your willingness and inner strength and begin to move through your day as you know you are capable. If it helps, pick one thing you are looking forward to, so that you can feel a sense of momentum and purpose. Every challenge in your day can be seen as something you need to overcome on your way to your destination— which could be anything: time with friends or family, a great meal, your favorite hobby. But the idea is that each day there is a mixture of things you *have* to do and things you *get* to do.

Many people will stumble here. It is completely normal to lack the motivation or confidence or calm or focus to wake up and just begin taking action. Even the most successful people have both good and bad days when they struggle to get going. No one has a tangible reason to believe in themself aside from their past successes; at first it is just a choice you make. If you find yourself in a slump, unable to find the self-belief to begin, remember this:

Your past holds a collection of everything you've overcome up to this point. It's proof that whatever happens in life, you can get through it, and if you can't, then you don't have to. Remind yourself that, "I can do this," or, "I'll be okay," and you will. Life only moves in one direction. Throughout history, we have had an incredible capacity to endure suffering because the human spirit holds a great desire to overcome.

Willpower is a defining human trait. It can co-exist with fear, doubt, exhaustion, or anything else that threatens to hold you back. Learn to dig deep and finish strong— the body and mind will quit long before the spirit. The willingness to move forward through the unknown, even when you don't feel your best, can make you beyond capable. In the last chapter, we discussed the idea that "vulnerability requires bravery, not certainty." The same is true for taking action. Life is not meant to be safe, without risk. Find your *why* for overcoming and you'll find the will to face your fear.

Other people will be stronger than you. Other people will be smarter than you. Other people will be born into better situations than you. But only you get to decide when your spirit and willpower quits. You decide how far you are willing to carry yourself.

As you continue to build your physical and mental foundation, you will get a sense for what you can practice along the way. First, maintaining physical health will help you to endure stressful periods of life. Then, consider the idea of "the mental gym": practicing present moment awareness, a willingness to face new challenges, self-belief, and the ability to let go of things outside your direct control. No one masters these practices all at once, and no one reaches a point of perfection. But if you can wake up and try, you will make progress and you will see yourself grow despite your fears.

Fear is paradoxical. To struggle with it, fight it. To overcome it, surrender to it. The goal is not to decrease fear, but rather to increase bravery. You are working to create an indomitable spirit in the face of uncertainty.

Be who you want to be despite all that you fear and all that could go wrong. Be honest with yourself and say, "What would I really want to do, if I weren't afraid?" And then go do that thing. You'll never know what you're capable of overcoming until you become willing to take risks. If your life is not what you want it to be, assume that no one else can change that except for you (thankfully, you will find people who want to help or support you along the way, but your life will always be your own responsibility). This is where happy, joyful people are so often misunderstood. In some cases, yes, ignorance is bliss. But for the most part, truly happy people see the same negativity and pain in the world as you do— they are just making a choice to be happy despite that truth. They embrace all of life with an attitude of acceptance and that, too, is a form of resilience and overcoming.

And finally, learn to trust that you are capable of facing the worst-case scenario. The subconscious wounds left by trauma are difficult to overcome because they often mean facing the full extent of your vulnerability. There is value in confronting your trauma once the danger has passed because you will eventually see all that you have overcome and maybe, you'll see how you kept going for that person inside you who originally got hurt. Stress strengthens the body and mind. What does traumatic stress create? An environment for you to become unstoppable by overcoming what seems impossible.

Painful and difficult events play out in life and they

are unavoidable. The greater tragedy may be the way we hold ourselves back from fully experiencing love and happiness after these events, when the threat is long gone. For many, this obstacle of "anxiety" is an evolved strength that is simply misunderstood. Thankfully, it can be trained.

7. TRAINING YOUR GUARD DOG

"Worry often gives a small thing a big shadow."

– Swedish proverb

The mind will seek out potential problems in your life, and it will continue to create new problems even if you have none.

Wait—*what?* Shouldn't the urge to find problems stop once you've solved the existing ones? That's just not how the mind likes to do its work. There is a Tibetan saying that "if you let your mind run wild, you will see a robber in an empty house." But how amazing is it that you have this mechanism in place to regularly look out for you? If left unchecked, the "anxiety" system can cause disorderly thinking, but when properly trained, you will feel the advantage of having a guard dog at your side.

Control issues and perfectionism are eventually born out of this need to continually solve problems. Do you have enough food, water, shelter, money, friendships and work? Good luck with your new set of unsolvable problems: politics, fear, existence, death and other forms of uncertainty that will *always* exist.

But we should take a step back. If you are at the point where you can worry about those sets of issues, your life is probably pretty fortunate, and to many, those worries would be considered a luxury. Depression and anxiety are often just a function of being unable to define when we are "enough" or have done "enough," or the very fear that we will not have "enough." Enough health, wealth, safety, competency… the object of your anxiety could be anything, but it generally follows the same theme: you don't have enough, and you need more, for some reason that you don't fully understand. But you just know you need more because this feeling is telling you so, and each time you follow that feeling, it gets stronger.

Thankfully, thoughts and feelings do not define you. Your mind is not your enemy and it will try hard to protect you, though you can defy it through your behaviors and actions. Whatever your worst fear may be, tell yourself "If it happens, I can handle it." It doesn't matter if it's rational, as fear and anxiety are often not, but you are teaching the mind that you are capable. Then, the mind will update its understanding of your world. This is how you build calm and confidence.

Recall in the first chapter, we began with the "lizard" and the "monkey" parts of our brain. These are just ideas, but they help with understanding the survival, emotional, and animal mechanisms that push us to make certain decisions, and they play a huge role in "anxiety" (as well as depression, which is closely related). For the lizard brain, we determined that, through the action of surrender, you could provide the necessary feedback that survival and safety have been attained, thereby aiding the regulation of this part of your brain. But the monkey is a bit more complex in its ability to process and understand fear and anxiety. You have to respect the input that the "monkey mind" provides you with— thoughts and feelings about your environment—but you do not always have to act on that input. You can make key decisions about whether or not to act, or react, based on knowing whether or not you have "enough."

In a future chapter, we will discuss the importance of defining "enough", but for now, you should understand the basic idea that it is crucial to regulating "anxiety" and finding peace. Recognize this, not as a permanent state, but as a resting point. For example, "I've done enough today," or, "I have enough today."

There is another point to address here: when "anxiety" becomes a component of your identity. Someone who *believes* that they are anxious or depressed would face an uphill battle. A belief is much stronger than a thought about something. To turn that around, and instead believe in yourself and your ability to move past these limitations, takes real courage. Your personality (and who you truly are at a human level) exists as something much greater than certain patterns of thought and behavior. No one who feels stuck is destined to remain stuck, thankfully, because of our innate ability to change and grow.

Worry only begins as a reaction but develops into a

habit. Stress can become addicting—and how do you beat any addiction? One day at a time of refusing to follow the compulsion. You can train this habit in either direction, and if you are pushed too far, it will escalate. If you reach a point of overwhelming anxiety and fear, then you might experience "panic." This is an important signal from your mind and body that it is time to slow down and take it easy. Panic is the mind saying, "I can't do this," and calm and capability represent the opposite state (which you build towards over time). These are reactions, emotions, and subjective states of mind which you can practice and learn in your own time, with a bit of patience and a lot of grace.

Instead of focusing on what you don't want to be (anxious, angry, reactive), help your mind by practicing what you want to be (calm, accepting, slow to react). That way, you become what you practice.

Again, the mind responds well to feedback loops. If you feel anxiety or fear despite the absence of any real threat, simply surrender to it and remain non-reactive. The mind takes this non-reaction as evidence that everything is fine, and then you begin to feel better naturally. This takes practice and is difficult, but exposure is the best way to retrain an overactive alert system. In that sense, the only way is "through" and while that may seem difficult, it is worthwhile because it will impact the rest of your life. The willingness to lean *into* fear is what will allow you to experience life fully.

Recognize that there will be real friction and effort in making these changes. When attempting to break unhelpful patterns of thought or behavior, remember the idea that "if it feels wrong, do it." Of course this is not an endorsement for wrongdoing, it just means that your mind may resist your attempt to break out of familiar patterns. But you will thank yourself in the future, as will everyone who came before you.

First, practice by staying calm through a stressful situation. Then, before you know it, you will begin to look forward to facing challenges and seeing yourself through them. You'll have more clarity and focus to set your mind after your next ambition, like a lion on a hunt. Stress will become expected and normal instead of defeating.

Your stress tolerance is a highly malleable threshold that can be moved and adjusted based on your response or reaction to stimulus. Use the analogy of a rusty wheel again. At first, stress seems overwhelming and grating. As you gradually practice by responding in a calm manner while keeping your breath, everything starts to loosen up and it becomes more natural to flow through stress and challenges. With your breathing, you can continue to handle higher levels of stress until what previously bothered you now seems small and insignificant. Of course, everyone needs breaks from stress and it is possible to get pushed too far.

In the worst-case scenario, you may find that a traumatic experience has left you in a state where the lizard, the monkey, and the guard dog all have control. You hide behind your guard dog, the monkey mind darts around from one thought to the next, and the lizard brain sees everything as life or death. When you experience something that is too overwhelming and difficult to understand, the mind creates constructs to protect you. But these extreme defense mechanisms don't usually serve you past a point. It's hard to return to being present when your mind is stuck on something that feels like *"What was that?"* An extreme memory becomes like bad food that you can't seem to digest. You become wired for crisis but woefully underprepared for peace and calm.

Ideally, you can find compassion after a traumatic experience in the form of love and support from others. If not, you have a bit more work to do by giving that compassion and understanding to yourself, so that you may return to homeostasis. You may be left feeling like you are anticipating the next bad thing that could happen in life. The release from that feeling comes from acceptance of the fact that you'll never know when the next challenge is coming, not the denial that it may happen. And now, you have the architecture in your mind to be even more prepared.

Remember that anxiety is an evolved mechanism meant to protect you, just like the immune system. The source of anxiety and fear is also the same source of tenacity and excitement. So, you do not want to remove this system; you just need to do your part to train or retrain it. Eventually, you may come to realize that you don't mind having this powerful defense mechanism.

So, what role then do *you* play in the management of your own mind? The guard dog will seek out real or perceived threats, and you will decide whether or not to react.

8. THE OBSERVER

*"To the mind that is still,
the whole universe surrenders."*

– Lao Tzu

There are minds that are running away from something, minds that are running towards something, and minds that are simply still, observing.

How do you typically feel on a given day? What recurring patterns of thought do you encounter most often? You can watch and observe these patterns that the mind creates. The most important thing to consider here: observation is a non-judgmental practice.

We all need compassion, but we also need to be responsible for how we feed our own pain. Taking full responsibility for yourself— your thoughts, feelings and actions— feels amazing because that is where personal growth begins. We should start there. Having the attitude of *I want to work on my life and get better at this* is all you need to get going, and it certainly helps to have self-awareness around your strengths and weaknesses, your thoughts and feelings, and where you wish to improve. Perfection is unattainable (and nothing is perfect in nature anyway), so instead, self-awareness becomes the goal. This will allow you to take smart action as you become self-aware through observation.

When you encounter difficult thoughts or feelings, stay present with them. Remain curious about them. Ride the wave and let them smoothen back into a state of calm. Getting good at feeling "bad" is a great skill that translates to feeling good without trying. See if you can relate to this example:

Feeling bad → Try hard to feel better → Begin to feel worse

So, try this instead:

Feeling bad → Acknowledge it, accept it; don't try to change it → Begin to feel better

Let the guard dog bark, then quiet on its own. All emotions serve as valid input and cannot be categorized as "bad" or "good" since they all serve a purpose. For example, stress and anxiety motivate you to take action. We are emotional beings who *can* use rational logic. Metaphorically, this is the animal that comes before the human. Don't deny your emotions; listen to them. You can listen with the goal of getting better at feeling rather than trying to feel better.

And remember, they are just thoughts and feelings. If you struggle against them you will simply reinforce their place in your mind. As you observe them, you can view them as just that and realize that there is great power in non-reactivity. As you remain curious, you can begin to wonder why you have many of these inputs in the first place. Many of the ones that you struggle with may have already served their purpose and you can probably trace them back to a past experience.

Acknowledging the presence of your thoughts and feelings is helpful, but you should be careful with giving them any real power. The more importance and meaning you place on them, the more they control you in return. The mind is an evolved tool for helping you live and navigate *this* world—the world outside your mind. When you regard your thoughts and feelings as less important than reality, it is easier to avoid getting caught up in them. And it is much easier to observe them and then to step back into the present moment. If you can observe your worries, you can also realize the fact that "worrying about *that* won't give me control over it."

To gain more control over yourself, and then your life, practice with how you respond to compulsions. Common inputs show up in our life: the compulsion to worry, to work more than you should, to eat when you're bored, to use media or news to avoid stress... Each time you decide not to respond to the compulsion, your executive control increases. This is roughly the same idea as the method that monks practice to become calm and quiet through meditation. They train their body and nervous system to be less reactive. They have top level executive control in their mind and in their ability to sit still as they watch thoughts and impulses come and go. They understand that there is nowhere to run and they can stay grounded.

There will always be a space between what happens and your subsequent reaction. See if you can master that space: relax your mind, then react. Don't react, then relax, because you'll have less control over your own reaction. The less you react, the more that space seems to grow. You can use this for any impulse or compulsion such as "I *have* to do this," or "I *have* to worry about this," or any of your initial reactions: hunger, anger, impatience, to name a few. See if you can hold off on your reaction and if you aren't sure what to do, do nothing. Your first impulse or reaction usually comes from your animal nature and does not result in the best outcome.

As you use this tool to regulate your thoughts and feelings, the "monkey mind" calms and everything begins to flow. This is just the first step to creating a sense of inner calm and peace as you become the observer of your own mind.

It's not easy all the time. Remember the first chapter that addressed how you begin with your animal nature and meeting basic needs, then you can try to live at the highest level as a human? Your body and mind are often trying to help you by giving you input and providing feedback on what you need. For that reason, sometimes you are just not going to feel calm until you get some much needed food, water, sleep or exercise. No one is perfect, but can you ground yourself and keep yourself as calm as possible, withholding any reaction or overreaction, until you're able to meet that basic need? After that, you might feel differently about how you wish to react.

Learn to observe these inputs and you will notice how things become a bit easier. Not every thought or feeling is helpful, but if you're curious, you might be able to understand yourself a bit better in the process. "Why do I think about *this* often? Why do I feel *this* way today?" It sounds simple, but it takes practice.

And if you find yourself overwhelmed with many things on your mind, find space to let them out. Write or talk. We are social animals and it is difficult to handle everything on your own, even if you become great at observing yourself. By creating separation between you and your thoughts, you give yourself some space to see them with a different perspective. Sometimes, you can let things go. In other situations, the solutions may come on their own. Or maybe a trusted friend will help you the same way that you would be willing to help them, without judgment.

At this point, you can begin to feel solid in your physical and mental foundation through an understanding of your core needs, a healthy relationship with your body, an attitude of acceptance, and a resilient and present mind. Connecting it back to the body, there are also biological benefits to being mindful and present. After all, it all starts at the top— the brain being the control center for the body. It's no great surprise that being calm is good for your health and well-being. In this mutual relationship between body and mind, what is good for one is also good for the other.

Trust yourself and practice your ability to stay in that present part of your mind, even when it's not easy.

You're going to feel that urge to run towards or away—don't. Hold on a bit and you'll be rewarded with a calm and present mind that helps you in every part of your life. There is no escape from whatever you are experiencing in the present moment, so it is worth learning how to live well in that moment.

How will you know if you're in a good place with your mental health? You'll know. You'll be accepting of the past, and excited about the future. You'll be present, and you'll know.

9. "ENOUGH"

"Gratitude is not only the greatest of all virtues, but the parent of all others."

– Cicero

You set the standards for your own life.

People spend a great deal of time questioning their own decisions and feeling unsure of the way they live their life, largely because we are social animals, so there is plenty of room for comparison. Available life advice is challenging to apply because it is not personalized to each individual. That being said, people generally go to therapy for two main reasons:

1) To tighten up
2) To loosen up

Obviously, the issues confronted in therapy are far more nuanced and complex than that, but that is the big picture idea. Half of the battle is categorizing yourself based on that criterion. And you can apply this logic to any part of your life while realizing that you don't need to be perfect to be successful.

Do you need intense exercise every day to be healthy? Of course not! But avoiding exercise altogether is obviously not ideal. It's important to find some balance between stress and rest.

Should you evaluate your mental health in every circumstance? Not at all. Stress is unavoidable and everyone needs some, but not too much. You manage stress over time and ideally, you don't overthink it.

Does it make sense to save every dollar while being as frugal as possible? No, then you aren't really leaving room for enjoyment. You still have to live your life. On the other hand, spending everything without a plan for saving can leave you unprepared for the future.

Ironically, people who work the hardest tend to be the least self-assured, which leads to more hard work, based on the feeling that they may not be doing "enough." People with lower work ethic may underestimate the value or impact of their efforts which then also leads to less action. These behaviors can exist in a cycle, either way.

How will you know if you exercise enough? If you eat well enough? If you worry too much or if you don't care enough? If you are saving or spending enough?

It's common to look around and notice what others

are doing. Should you always listen to advice from people who tell you "what" you need to do? Not necessarily. Following someone else's advice can lead you to become too loose or too tight with your health, mental well-being or wealth, if you don't know your own nature. There is a tendency to look towards successful people in the hope that you can follow their advice and then emulate their lifestyle and this does make sense in certain situations, but the problem is that you aren't living their life. It's your life. Your set of goals and circumstances may look completely different from what another person wishes to accomplish. So, feel free to follow someone else's advice on "what" to do, but you will find it more fulfilling to follow your own path instead.

The best answers you will find are inside you.

If you are reading this book, you understand that the goal is to trust yourself and make your own way. You can borrow from other people's expertise and you can value the advice from someone who has mastered a particular area of life, but copying their every behavior is unnecessary. You don't have to live up to someone else's standard unless your goal is to please them. Conventional success by societal standards is, unsurprisingly, dissatisfying to most. For your life, you define success in your own terms.

Defining your personal "enough" is a key skill in any area of life, but especially in wealth.

Do you want to become truly wealthy or does it make the most sense to focus on getting out of debt, first? There are important questions you need to ask while being realistic about your life and what is possible. Everyone has a different starting point and similar to quality health and mental well-being, financial success should be viewed as an ongoing journey.

Happiness and life satisfaction are largely subjective. What does that tell us? That the parameters which dictate your happiness are the ones you decide on. Two people in the same circumstances can have a different outlook on life— one person can feel incredibly grateful, while another person feels like they are still struggling for more. It is often just a matter of perspective and the ability to define what is really "enough."

Recall from earlier that the mind will help you to seek out and solve problems in your life, but then it will continue to try to find or create problems, even when there are none. This becomes unsustainable at the point when you cannot define "enough" for yourself and you are unable to find satisfaction and appreciation for what you have accomplished so far.

Set your own goals and decide exactly what makes you happy. Whether it is luxury or simple pleasures, you can't make clear progress without a specific goal in mind. Sometimes, "enough" is a moving target that has more to do with where you are today versus where you are hoping to end up tomorrow. You may even begin to judge your success in life based on the actions you take, the process you choose to follow, and the feeling that you are not doing "too little" or "too much." It is satisfying to find yourself in balance.

Next, we will explore the most sustainable mindset for achieving financial (or any other form of) success.

10. MONTHLY MAGIC

*"We first make our habits,
then our habits make us."*

– John Dryden

A section on wealth may feel a bit out of place in this book, but resource management will always play a fundamental role in our lives. Good physical and mental health are paramount, but healthy habits around wealth are a critical piece of our foundation due to the way that we interact with our world every day. It is very common to have too little or too much and to stay stuck in unhealthy patterns that no longer serve you. There is a reason why you focus on creating discipline in your mental and physical habits first, before you can begin to apply similar ideas to your finances. That being said, most people are closer than they realize to being financially successful.

Consistent success is built out of patterns and routine, and wealth functions no differently.

Common obstacles in the way of financial health include: lack of opportunity, being stuck in survival mode, short-term thinking, believing that "this isn't for me," overspending or oversaving, distrust in financial institutions, fear of loss, and lack of education.

Sometimes, it is enough to address the gap in any of these given areas. In most situations, you have to accept the current limitations and then begin to work towards what is realistically possible. For others, you must consider whether or not you are doing too much and have become "too tight", which presents its own problems. Either way, this is why you established an attitude of acceptance, resilience and willpower leading up to this point. There is a great deal that you cannot control about your situation, but that does not mean you lack influence over your future. This applies with the body, the mind, and it is definitely the case for wealth.

The challenge of becoming wealthy can seem overwhelming, so just start small. Begin by getting everything in your life organized. Everything is more difficult when you are disorganized and that will always be true. Regardless of whether you earn much or little, efficiency in your accumulation of wealth will depend largely on your ability to keep track of details. With some awareness about your starting point, you can begin to evaluate and make decisions.

Do you have clear and specific goals in mind?
Can you define which expenses are absolutely necessary, and which are not?

Are you spending too much or possibly too little?
What changes are you comfortable with making?
Do you need to learn more about how to allocate your resources?

Questions and curiosity will help here as you take stock of your current situation. Then, with the information you have gathered, it's time to make decisions about where you want to go. We'll use the analogy of the rusty wheel here, yet again. Resource management is most difficult in the beginning as you make changes and establish new habits, but it becomes automatic over time. The mind adapts pretty well to lifestyle changes in either direction when you decide to spend more or less—new habits become the default and, after a period of adjustment, the mind sees this is the norm.

Accumulating wealth and financial security happens the same way that you build a healthy body or a strong mind: repeatable and sustainable habits. Usually, you don't need a big break— you need small amounts of consistency over a period of time.

Try using an amount of time to budget and repeat these habits— days, weeks and especially months, work best. You can plan using years, but this is far less predictable, due to the nature of change in life. You'll find that your habits become second nature when they feel sustainable and repeatable. And then the magic happens— days become weeks, become months, and then finally become years of compounding financial success.

With rare exception, consistency is the surest path to wealth and security. Find what feels sustainable. Have a plan and do your best to stick to it. Focus on process over results. You start small and build over time and the results are almost always surprisingly good when the habits and process are good, as well. Your budget and actions may only play out month by month, but after three, four, or five years? You'll get to look back and see all that you've accomplished. A financial goal that is five, ten or twenty years away may seem daunting, but the secret lies in being consistent during the days, weeks, and months that you live and operate.

Do the small things that allow you to feel good about each day, while setting yourself up for a successful future.

At the end of the day, long-term financial success is determined by how you pay yourself. There are many, many possible paths to accomplish this, but the idea is that it has far more to do with what you save rather than what you earn. That is likely one of the greatest misconceptions about financial success: the idea that you must earn a lot to accumulate wealth. Many people will get stuck on that belief and it will prevent them from trying in the first place. These self-limiting beliefs show up everywhere—in health, mental well-being, and finance—and are simply not true in reality. There are always going to be factors outside of your control, but where you end up in the future is going to be heavily dictated by the choices you make today.

Lastly, it is helpful if you can develop a comfort with taking calculated risks. This is true in every area of life, but especially in your career and wealth. There is no need to be brazen by taking unnecessary and excessive risks in an attempt to become financially successful. But at times, it will benefit you to take a step back in order to take a larger step forward, and it helps if you have conditioned your mind to accept risk and uncertainty. Any investment is a decision to give something up today with the expectation that it will pay off in the future. This takes discipline and delayed gratification, but it is worthwhile when you realize that you are creating your future through actions in the present.

As you maintain healthy habits and see your success compound and grow over time, check in with yourself and evaluate whether or not you are doing "enough."

11. LIVING GUILT-FREE

"No valid plans for the future can be made by those who have no capacity for living now."

– Alan Watts

So often, we choose to keep going and going without pausing to recognize what we have accomplished thus far. We build and hustle without reflection or thought. How will you measure your own progress if you do not stop and look back on how far you've come?

Let's say that by this point, you understand the importance of doing your best and creating healthy habits for your body, mind, and resources. Self-improvement is great. Growth is valuable. But what magical indicator will tell you when you have done "enough?" Other people may recognize your hard work, but no one will come along and tell you to stop. The downside of seeking constant self-improvement and growth is that you send the signal to yourself that you aren't good enough— it's an unrelenting focus on every negative or perceived "lacking" in your life. There are dangerous implications that stem from constantly seeking more, as we will discuss in a future chapter around hedonism, but for now, we will focus on how this applies to financial success.

Wealth will only ever be a means to an end. If money is your end goal, that is an incomplete thought process because you cannot take it with you when you die.

Of course, it feels good to be prepared for the future, but you don't live in the future. Spending it all today, conversely, sets you up for failure down the line.

We gather resources for peace of mind and relief from the fear that we might not have "enough." Almost everything we do is centered around the quest for pleasure or the avoidance of pain, but without any tool for measurement, we become lost in the process of "seeking" while never necessarily "finding." This is the importance of deciding on what is "enough" and then recognizing when you are in rhythm. So the question becomes: how do you find a balance?

It's okay to have goals and to strive for more in your life. But the challenge that arises is when happiness and peace of mind are always somewhere off in the future, never to be found where you are today. If you decide not to take responsibility for your life and its direction, then it may not improve in any measurable way. If you focus only on doing or acquiring more, then you will inevitably burn out. Invest in the future, uncertain as it may be, but live for today.

You are not in competition with anyone else. Have you been taking better care of your body lately? With practice, do you feel more accepting, resilient and generally centered in life? Are you improving your habits around saving or spending in a way that better aligns with your values?

Celebrate your progress along the way! None of the hard work matters if you can't slow down enough to enjoy it.

Surely, there will be more challenges ahead, but you'll want to notice when things are simply going well. It can be tough to fully appreciate this after a stressful period in life, but it is worthwhile. Picture the spider when its web is knocked down. Despite what has happened, it looks, not to the outcome, but to its efforts to keep rebuilding. It determines that there is still hope for the future and it is worth trying to create a life in the face of adversity.

If you are reading this book, trying to improve your life, and working to improve the lives of others, the only thing that really counts is that effort. You don't control the outcome. A good process usually does lead to favorable outcomes, but it does not give you control. Instead, look at your life, recognize your own efforts and see if you can't find peace in *that*.

The whole point of building your foundation is to allow you to experience life fully. You will get knocked off balance from time to time, but you'll know exactly how to find your footing again. Then, you can build off of that to find success and fulfillment in your relationships and daily life. It all starts with the willingness to take responsibility for yourself and all that you have overcome up to this point. So, it is worth recognizing.

Congrats on making it this far.

Section II: Relational Needs

12. KNOW YOURSELF IN OTHERS

*"Each friend represents a world in us,
a world not born until they arrive,
and it is only by this meeting that a new world is born."*

– Anais Nin

Do you feel like certain people just don't get *it*?

If you aren't sure what *it* is— that feeling that there is something you are seeing that other people aren't, some area where you just fail to connect with others, or maybe an idea about how things could be better. *It* represents the unique lens through which you view reality. You aren't meant to be fully understood by everyone. And you certainly don't need to spend time convincing others that your way of seeing the world is the "right" way, nor do you need to adopt the views of others. What is valuable, instead, is seeking out relationships where you can develop a mutual understanding.

Independence is useful to develop, but everyone relies on others in this world. You need both. In any relationship, the opposite of loneliness is a deep understanding between people.

Think about any of your closest relationships. In some ways, they represent a reflection of all or part of your personality. There is an overlap in interests, hobbies, passions, personal philosophy, humor, or goals. That overlap will likely never be perfect because everyone has a different set of experiences, but some amount of difference is favorable for creating healthy conflict and growth. Through interactions with friends, or even strangers, it is fascinating to see what aspects of your personality come through. We have a natural desire to connect with people who see the world the same way that we do (and interestingly, most humans do care about the same things at a basic level).

Valuable connection and understanding are fostered through vulnerable communication. Earlier in this book, we explored the idea of developing connection by listening to the body. The same idea can be applied in relationships. Consider this example, which you may have experienced before:

When listening to a friend as they share their problems, you can feel a solution come to mind as they are speaking. You are excited to be able to help and give them an answer—you've experienced this problem before, figured it out, and you know it's no big deal. But here's the main issue: they may not be interested in solutions yet, even if you can feel that you have a great answer in mind. They are likely just looking to be understood.

Most people want to feel supported to find their own solutions and feel capable in their ability to get there. As a good friend, you can listen and support this process and when you listen carefully, you might understand and feel what your friend is going through as if it were you experiencing it.

In listening and communicating, there is a give and take that represents the nature of vulnerability. Two sides that are both "open." It is meant to feel mutual rather than one-sided and through that process, you develop connection and understanding. Unfortunately, these things don't seem to function at the same level if you aren't willing to be open and vulnerable, or if you aren't able to give as much as you take.

Seek out and find people with whom you can create this understanding and balance. You'll know the feeling when you really connect with someone naturally, you shouldn't have to force it. Hopefully, you will meet people who bring out the best in you and allow you to express yourself fully. The advice here is *not* to only have relationships with people who agree with you and align with you on everything—we all need to be challenged in healthy ways in order to grow—but you do want to be able to share connection and understanding while maintaining mutual respect.

Occasionally, you will pick up on a glimmer of your own being in someone else. Maybe it's in their humor or the way they think about life. When you sense that, open that door and walk through it. That is a genuine opportunity to connect more deeply and to foster a greater relationship. It feels exciting when someone has an idea and you recognize, "Hey, I've thought about that before, too!"

And if the people in your life now are focused on topics or ideas that you can't seem to relate to? *That's okay.* It is likely a sign that you have changed and grown and you will need to practice one of two things:

1) Share your interests and see if people meet you halfway.
2) Connect with new people who understand you more.

Your relationships should enhance, not detract from, the way you experience life. If you can tell that a relationship feels one-sided, it may be time to reconsider what purpose that relationship serves in your life. It's okay to re-evaluate that and let go of a relationship at the point when it is no longer healthy. Just because something feels familiar, does not mean it is right for you.

While you shouldn't live to please others, you also shouldn't live to prove other people wrong. Instead, aim to prove yourself and the people who believe in you right. Those are the people who care for you unconditionally, and they are the ones you will want to have along for your journey.

13. THE IMPORTANCE OF UNCONDITIONALITY

"I think modern medicine has become like a prophet offering a life free of pain. It is nonsense. The only thing I know that truly heals people is unconditional love."

– Elisabeth Kübler-Ross

It is more than important—it is vital—to develop self-compassion; to be understanding of your mistakes and shortcomings; to consider yourself as someone who is doing their best, given the circumstances. It will affect your well-being, your health and your ability to face life on life's terms. The kindness you deny yourself will inevitably affect those around you.

Maybe you are hard on yourself because someone else was hard on you when you struggled. Maybe you think you don't deserve love because someone denied you of it when you needed it most. Sometimes, the negative voice in your head is not yours at all— it is an artifact from a time when someone let you down. Self-love is not egotistical, it is necessary.

Do you care about the well-being of others? Are you capable of loving someone else? Can you think of another person, right now, who you love? If you answered "yes" to any of these questions, it is a guarantee that other people would answer the same while thinking of you. Step back for a moment and try to see yourself objectively:

You come into this world and your parents try to do their best with raising you, but they don't completely know what they're doing. They probably get *some* things wrong because no one is perfect and life is messy. You have strange and confusing experiences as you age and learn to fit in with people around you. Before you know it, you're an adult now trying to function in our society and just like your parents, you also don't fully know what you're doing. But you know that you're doing your best and trying to figure it out. For what it's worth, you didn't ask to be here! Your parents made you and brought you into this world and now you're here, trying to make the most of it. All you know is that you wake up each day and try again. You just keep going.

Loving yourself means accepting *that* person—the person who didn't turn out perfect, who doesn't understand everything, and who feels unsure of themselves now and then. That person is you and, no surprise; it is also everyone else around you, no matter how they appear on the outside. Life can be a special, lottery-ticket experience to find meaning and happiness for some, but for most, it involves a great deal of pain and struggle. That truth alone means that you deserve some amount of grace and others do, too.

Learn how to give yourself unconditional love and you will unlock new layers of your being. It may feel unnatural at first—some of us choose to be hard on ourselves because we believe it fuels us to work harder—but you might find that accepting and supporting yourself leads to an even greater strength through self-belief. Then, when you need to reset, it becomes easier to accept yourself and your past while focusing on what you can do, moving forward. You don't waste your energy; that form of strength doesn't run out of stamina.

Unfortunately, people with bad intentions (or sometimes just lacking in their own self-love) can often detect when you lack the ability to give yourself unconditional love and kindness. The danger here is that this leaves you open to being manipulated, as someone else aims to fill that void in an effort to get what they need. Learn to love and accept yourself before you love someone else.

A relationship between two healthy and independent people will always fare better than a relationship where one or both people lack independence. In every relationship, romantic or otherwise, there is an exchange which should feel at least somewhat mutual. The better the understanding and communication between two people, the more mutual the relationship can become. That is why early chapters in this book focus on building your individual foundation first.

Loneliness is so difficult for any creature, but it should

not drive you towards the wrong relationships. Even when you are alone, you can think of others and understand that this is a large and bustling world with so many other people out there. With a bit of patience, you'll find yourself surrounded by the right ones.

You have a responsibility to make sure that you are being treated in a healthy way, while understanding that you can't change how others may act. How can you be yourself around people who do not accept you as you are? The treatment you allow from others is an unconscious reflection of your self-worth. That may feel like a big responsibility but it is part of growing into an emotionally healthy adult. You have a right to choose who you want in your life, and the more people you meet, the more you will realize that there are people out there who will treat you the way you want to be treated. You can seek out those relationships and work to maintain them.

Understand this: love is given, never owed.

A relationship is not a function of ownership, but one of balance and respect. Your family, friendships and romantic relationships should hopefully reflect this mutual love, respect, and acceptance. If you can work towards that over time, then you will feel your self-worth grow. That decision, to seek the best kind of treatment, is one you make out of an unconditional love for yourself.

14. TEND TO YOUR ROOTS

*"Don't walk behind me; I may not lead.
Don't walk in front of me; I may not follow.
Just walk beside me and be my friend."*

– Albert Camus

There are striking similarities between humans and trees. The way we lay down "roots," form connections, and maintain them for a longer and healthier life. Relationships represent living, breathing connections which require regular attention and care.

A great deal of life satisfaction is derived from the quality of your relationships as well as your ability to think of others. And you aren't alone. Many animals struggle with loneliness and isolation. Most people also know the pain of losing a family member, a friend, or a lover. There is nothing wrong with spending time alone, but we are wired to be together. How you manage your relationships throughout your life will affect far more than you realize. While the last two chapters discussed how healthy relationships can benefit your life, this chapter deals more with the importance of caring for those connections.

How did it feel the last time that you shared something important with someone, only to realize that their attention drifted off while you were speaking?

Attention is a gift to another person. In that sense, listening is not only about what you gain but also about what you give. It's about giving the other person a voice that matters. Listen, digest what the other person has said, and *then* share your response. This practice changes the nature of each conversation and each party gains more.

It's normal to be tired or preoccupied and to miss what someone was attempting to convey to you. Nevertheless, people can tell when you aren't entirely present and it feels a bit defeating for the person who is trying to be heard. No one is a perfect listener, so it's going to happen now and then, but over time, too many of these missed opportunities will cause communication to decline. Remember, vulnerable communication helps to keep two people feeling connected. Without it, the relationship erodes.

Just ask people about *them*. It's fun. You never know what they'll say and it's enjoyable to explore another person's thoughts on anything really.

There are many recipes for a healthy relationship, but most will probably require some combination of:

Communication + Attention + Trust + Effort

A lack in any one of these areas will cause the relationship— the living connection— to fade over time. Think of a friend who you haven't spoken to in a while. You may not be able to *feel* them in the same way that you feel the person who sits across from you now, or a friend that you saw yesterday. But you can check on your friends or loved ones, anytime, just to maintain that connection. You can relieve some amount of your own loneliness by reaching out to remind another person that they matter.

Compassion is a human superpower. And more importantly, it is contagious. It is the ability to look at someone and make them feel like they are really there, they matter, and they are "enough."

There will be times when a person you care about finds themself feeling down. In those moments, compassion helps us to connect and cultivate healthy relationships. Don't underestimate what kindness can mean to another person, even a stranger. Making a positive impact on someone else causes a ripple effect of positive change in the world, and you never know when you might be rescuing another person from their lowest point. And it's not only about being there for someone when they are down. Encourage your friends and get excited for them in their brightest moments. It costs you nothing and it puts even more wind behind their sails. Joy can be shared in a relationship even through one person's success.

Most healthy friendships can persist through disagreements and time apart, but romantic relationships need to be managed with particular care and attention. This can be all too easy to forget once you find yourself in the flow of everyday routine, failing to notice someone who once seemed like the most important person in the world—the person right across from you.

Love is thrilling in the beginning and, by comparison, "boring" during the relationship. And that's a good thing! Stability is where you can build something special. Find someone who makes you feel calm and allows you to be yourself.

It's not easy to share such a close bond with any human being. Every human is difficult in their own way and there are no perfect matches that make for a seamless, carefree relationship without any amount of conflict. But it's worth trying. Growth happens through healthy conflict and vulnerable communication… and then comes the opportunity to build a romantic relationship with deep understanding and respect. You can experience life with someone who will face the world with you.

Ultimately, conflict is inevitable in any relationship, but can be navigated skillfully with the right mindset. During or after an argument, take an honest look at yourself and determine: what was your responsibility in that situation? If you can identify that, you can acknowledge your part and bridge the gap to keep up good communication in a relationship. Try to use your imagination—you can put yourself in the other person's situation for just a moment, to understand what might *really* be bothering them. If you can speak to that, it will be far easier to find common ground.

Managing relationships is a skill that takes practice—*every day* practice. But it is one of the most rewarding aspects of being alive. Our ability to connect, bond, create, and procreate with others is central to what fulfills us in life, both at an animal and human level. We all long to be part of something larger than ourselves.

15. ONE IN EIGHT BILLION

"I guess we all like to be recognized not for one piece of fireworks, but for the ledger of our daily work."

– Neil Armstrong

The food you eat…

The clothes you wear…

The bed you sleep on…

Your phone, your computer, your company…

None of it can exist without the people around you. Our combined efforts allow the world to function, not in perfect harmony, but in a complex and intricate network. Small actions and decisions have a surprisingly significant impact on our world at large. It would be a gross misunderstanding to say that any effort or contribution, no matter how trivial, simply "doesn't matter." It is impossible to escape the interconnectedness of our world.

Imagine a day when you don't feel like working. You wake up and can't seem to find the motivation or desire but you know it's something you *have* to do. You make the choice to get working anyway, and you end up having a decent day. Nothing goes wrong, but nothing particularly exciting happens either. You showed up, you did your part—end of story.

But then, imagine another world where you decide it's not worth it to work that day. You determine that it is inconsequential and no one would really notice, anyway. It shouldn't really impact anything. The day passes and you decide you will try again the next day.

What is the difference between these two scenarios? You are only one person, after all, so it probably shouldn't matter. The difference is that *something* did not happen.

Well, that much is obvious and not the least bit profound. But you can't identify what exactly did not happen. Maybe someone else was unable to get the help that they needed. Or perhaps you missed an exciting opportunity with your manager, a seemingly unimportant conversation with a colleague, progress on your work was slowed by that day which then delayed others. As we zoom out, we begin to see the ripple effect of change in our world caused by one small decision which then leads to something much larger.

The point of this idea is not that you should work every day without time off; instead, it demonstrates your impact and value:

Your contributions in life are important, no matter how big or small. They help to keep the world moving forward.

Humility can be found in the recognition that our personal struggle in life is not unique. Thankfully, life is never about one person as much as many would like to imagine it that way.

Our human world is largely built on shared growth and progress. Imagine if everyone who did not necessarily feel like doing their part just decided instead to pass on their responsibilities. We cannot fully function without each other—at least not on the highest level as a healthy society—and you should not underestimate your individual part in this globally interconnected system. You never have to feel like everything depends on you alone. Thankfully, much has happened and many have come before you just to bring you to this point.

We have a tendency to find ourselves in the present, looking back on everything that has led us to this moment, while believing that everything which previously happened can explain how we got here. What if we looked forward with that same attitude and mindset? That is influence, not control. The work you do today will impact your tomorrow (and likely everyone else's tomorrow, too). It's okay if your job today isn't the one that you want for the rest of your life—that is perfectly normal and most people won't spend their whole life working only on their passions. But you *can* believe in the change that exists in the future, as well as your ability to contribute to it today.

Success in life is a function of two things: hard work and opportunity. You cannot succeed without both. Many people are far more fortunate than others to receive better opportunities. But many others will squander great opportunities while failing to apply the hard work. Making your own way means making the most of your individual opportunities, whatever they may be.

Your purpose in life may not be only one thing, but you might find part or all of it in your work and societal contributions. Or, maybe you work just to make the rest of your life possible which is great, too. Whatever your reason, it is important to see how it connects you to everyone else in the world. And apart from purpose, anyone can benefit from spending their working hours or free time in a way that challenges them and helps them grow.

16. EXERCISE YOUR MIND

"…a mind needs books as a sword needs a whetstone, if it is to keep its edge."

– Tyrion Lannister (from George R.R. Martin's *Game of Thrones*)

People who age well tend to have a number of things in common: strong relationships, good physical health, a sense of purpose, and above all else… a sharp mind.

Just like the body, the mind needs stress and rest. The mind loves to help with identifying and solving problems, but it also needs idle time. Don't underestimate the value of even one, two, five, or ten minutes of time in which your mind is not actively working on *something*. This will leave you feeling refreshed and ready for more.

The mind is a capable and willing "problem solver" and it enjoys something that is challenging, but not too far out of its comfort zone. In general, we ask our minds to do a lot for us. Anxiety and burnout occur with overuse of your greatest resource, or when your mind gets stuck on a perceived problem that is outside of your control. Trying to tackle an unsolvable problem will land you in a space of thinking in loops.

For this, there is an antidote: never lose your ability to find your way back to the present. Present moment awareness allows for a greater connection to all things living in this moment at the same time as you. Beyond that, it will help you in countless situations but especially in times of crisis. Sustained attention and focus are resources that can be trained with practice. They are not unlimited, but their capacity can expand or contract.

Aside from avoiding or managing the situations that trouble the mind, it is worth asking: what specifically sharpens it?

Reading, learning, writing, playing music, exercising, deep conversations, or any other activity or hobby that you can fully engage in are key. There are many possibilities and the answer is unique to you. Think of ways that you can immerse yourself, gently challenging your mind without overstraining.

These activities all have one thing in common—you cannot be effective at them while your mind is elsewhere. When you start reading a book, your attention may drift off several times before you become focused. In the middle of your exercise, can you stay present? Previously, we discussed the benefits of being a good, attentive listener and how it benefits your relationships. Find the challenges that you enjoy which also allow you to let go of everything else except what you are doing in the present moment, and then keep at it.

Passive activities help the mind to rest and reset, while focused activities require mental effort. The mind is a lot like the body in this way—"use it or lose it." Many people who remain sharp despite their age are often doing the same challenging mental exercises that they did when they were younger. They never stopped using their mind.

They also make a concerted effort to "keep up" as times change. Given that our world is ever evolving, it makes sense to keep an open mind for continued learning and engagement. It becomes more difficult once you are closed off to new information.

This is the real value of ongoing learning: as people age, they either become more confident in incorrect beliefs or they become humble in knowing that they are simply getting less "wrong" over time. The more confident you are in a fixed belief or piece of information, the more you limit your ability to learn and grow. Challenge your mind's desire to be absolutely "certain" and instead, approach life with the attitude that you know little, but are capable of learning a great deal. Like any tool, you can sharpen your mind on new information, each and every day.

Up to this point, you built a foundation of quality physical, mental and financial habits. Then, you determined the importance of maintaining a healthy relationship with yourself, the people around you, and finally, with your work and societal contributions. Recall the chapter about living in a way that is "guilt-free?" The same ideas apply here in the way that you choose to spend your free time. Everyone knows their time is limited, but they do not necessarily apply that truth in their life.

17. THE ART OF SPENDING TIME

"Time you enjoy wasting is not wasted time."

– Marthe Troly-Curtin

There is a reason we begin with habits and a healthy foundation: discipline and routine create a lot of freedom in life. The mind loves shortcuts and routine gives you less to think about while you focus on bigger things in your life.

Ask yourself a simple question: Where do you find your release?

Exploring this will yield some interesting results. For many, it is substances. For others, it is media, junk food, or something else that is difficult to put down. Some will realize that they don't currently have a release and should probably find a healthy one. Identify these patterns in your life and then free yourself by redirecting them to other sources (of course, you don't need to be perfect. You should still enjoy things that aren't "good" for you as long as they aren't derailing your life.) Books, movies, music, sports, writing, art, time with friends, exercise, reflections on good memories, and quality food can all be substitutes, to name a few.

The object of your spent time is not the point. Hobbies are an expression of your personality and interests, after all, but humans do tend to have "common denominators" for what generally feels good. There is a fullness and richness to life that you can't help but experience on a day when you move your body, eat good food, have an interesting conversation, and enjoy some time with your favorite hobby. Hopefully, by this point you have a better understanding of your baseline needs—physically, mentally, financially, socially, etc—and you can satisfy what you need to make the most of any given day. Only you know what this "perfect day" looks like because only you understand how you like to spend your precious time.

The issue with looking to others for what to do is that there is no "right" way to live life; there's only your way (as long as it doesn't involve harming or exploiting others, obviously). What do you find relaxing? How would you build your life, ideally? If you base your standards on what everyone else is doing, you will find yourself disappointed somewhere down the road. Your outer world will end up in direct conflict with your inner world, and you will realize that you are living the wrong life, for you.

Don't be afraid to try something new even if it defies the conventions set in place by others. Break the rules, as long as it doesn't hurt anyone else—anything can seem unusual, until you do it.

And there is nothing wrong at all with "wasting time" —sometimes, you recharge to keep going. It doesn't make sense to always busy yourself, just for the sake of being busy. The Italians have a saying, "*il dolce far niente*," which translates to "the sweetness of doing nothing." Can you apply that in your own life? How often do you allow yourself to relax and let everything simply "be"? This is the nature of "guilt-free" time, knowing that you are already doing "enough" in other areas of your life. So, you can make time for "being" instead.

While we previously discussed the idea of knowing yourself through how you interact with others, solitude is a different way to get to know yourself. No one is freer than when they are alone. We are social animals and we do need connection, but the time spent connecting with yourself is great, too. You can enjoy any of your favorite hobbies and catch up on everything that's been on your mind.

Thinking about life is interesting and important, but it should not be confused with the verb or the action of living life. Thinking, reflecting, and reframing are all done with the purpose of having a healthier mindset to enjoy life even more, without having to think as much.

Is there a better feeling than letting yourself fully sink into, well, anything? The world disappears and it's just you, your mind, and the task at hand. You are immersed in a way that you almost become one with the activity, the challenge, or the conversation. You enjoy your particular affinity for what's in front of you.

The opposite feeling of anxiety, towards anything, is capability—"I can do this," or even better, "I'm skilled at doing this." We are survivors, adventurers, and creators as we have been since the beginning of time. One person might go hiking and camping out in the woods but another person will derive satisfaction from finishing a creative project—the goal is to find that sweet spot in what you find enjoyable, engaging, entertaining, and challenging enough to hold your attention.

And finally, always make time for humor. Humor is so incredibly essential to keeping your spirits high and it can be hard to find in challenging times, but it's just as necessary. There is a reason all people can relate through play and laughter.

Why is it so important to consider how you spend your free time? It's the same question as asking why you exercise, take care of your mind, and pay your bills. You should never lose sight of this personal reason for being. It's part of why you get up to do anything. If you can directly tie the work or effort to the reward, it will become far easier to find motivation to get through anything. Looking forward to a relaxing dinner with friends? You can get through each obstacle between now and then, no problem. The more regularly you relate your "overcoming" to everything else in your life, the more it all starts to make sense. Remember, we evolved with a daily mix of things we *have* to do and things we *get* to do. Connecting these two will make the latter even more rewarding.

Finding time for everything is a real challenge, but let's say that you reach a point where you feel good about taking care of your body, mind, and resources. You're connecting with people, finding value in your work, and enjoying your free time. Through your relationships, work and life experiences, you will accumulate knowledge of our world. From the day that you are born, you have an innate ability, so powerful that it often occurs at the subconscious level. You learn lessons; you define your experiences.

You have the incredible ability to take life and from it: *make* your own meaning.

Section III: Spiritual Needs

18. *TETSUGAKU*

"Even monkeys fall from trees."

– Japanese proverb

Here we are at somewhat of an intermission. The journey to fulfillment and self-actualization has everything to do with our ability to first feel safe and secure within ourselves, then connected and valued in our communities. Only after these needs are met can you reflect on life and create meaning from your experiences.

Ancient philosophies enjoy a timeless relevance in our modern world. Humans have tried for a very long time to distill our experience of reality into ideas that make sense for living life in a practical manner. What is *most* interesting is how humans across the world have already shared many of the same thoughts about life, even going back hundreds or thousands of years. This is a shared experience—the way that people live, work, feel joy and pain and love and loss, and then ultimately experience death. People have always wondered what it all means, but life's inherent meaning is highly unique from person to person because the lens through which you experience reality can be shifted or distorted significantly by your experiences.

Many cultures value the idea of experiencing life with a certain calm and inner stillness (think: The Observer). The Japanese, among others, deserve to be recognized for their teachings in this area. Their philosophies are profound, but simple. While each philosophy has its own distinct meaning, we are going to apply several ideas loosely in the context of this book and what has been discussed so far:

Uketamo — Humble acceptance

The goal in developing an attitude of acceptance is to flow through life more effortlessly. This will make you stronger, not weaker. Rather than wishing for things to be perfect, understand that peace and joy are found in appreciating what is. Conversely, you will continue to feel dissatisfaction as long as you wish for life to be anything besides what it is. You can still dream of change and take action to bring it to life, but acceptance means that you see the bumps in the road and you move forward while doing your best to enjoy the journey. It is important to accept life with all its warts and bruises because there is always a great deal of happiness at stake.

Kaizen — Continuous improvement

Self-improvement is achieved through a focus on process rather than results. Most favorable outcomes stem from having a good, consistent process. Physical, mental and financial health are created through regular habits and progress matters more than perfection. Are you finding new ways to grow? If you balance the desire for new growth with the appreciation of how far you've already come, it becomes easier to continue moving forward with a willingness to keep getting better.

Gaman — Perseverance

Believe in your ability to endure and overcome. Historically, humans have dealt with failure and disaster, but we make the choice to keep going, for the sake of our loved ones and our goals in life. Willpower is essential to the human spirit. It's the last thing you can fall back on when all else seems lost. When your body is tired and the mind begins questioning how you are going to do something, you can trust in your ability to persevere and make it through as many people have before you.

Kintsugi — Embrace your flaws

Feeling better and becoming more effective as a person begins with self-awareness and an acceptance of your strengths and weaknesses. Oftentimes, your greatest strength is formed out of your greatest weakness and vice versa. You can't necessarily have one and not the other. Embrace this part of being human. It is not necessary nor possible to perfect yourself and remove all of your weaknesses; instead, you simply need to remain aware of your struggles in life and build around them. Everyone else has them too and it works both ways—the more you accept in yourself, the more easily you accept others.

Zazen — Sitting meditation

Better understanding of your thoughts and feelings can be achieved through non-judgmental observation. This is quite difficult when you are tangled up in your mind; so, try to create a bit of space and separation. If a friend were struggling with a certain thought or feeling, you would ask them, "Why?" Observation is the same practice but within ourselves.

Ikigai — Your reason for living

You are able to create your own purpose through your values, goals, and actions. This is a key part of what makes life meaningful—seeing yourself as capable while realizing that your contributions to the world are valuable. Your purpose and your reason for being can involve anything: work, friends, family, your favorite hobby, or all of these combined. What challenge or effort brings you satisfaction and joy? Define that and you'll know more about your purpose.

Ichigo Ichie — Living in the moment

Your life is a unique journey. While it will resemble others, you are the first person to walk this exact path. Enjoy your time and pay attention in the moment. You can work hard, prepare for the future, and make exciting plans, but it will all fall flat if you fail to find yourself fully present and open to experiencing the moment. If you pay close attention, there are many special coincidences and magical moments in life. The more present you become, the better your intuition for life.

Wabi-Sabi — Accept life's impermanence and imperfections

Look at life and realize: you don't have to figure it all out today. Everything you experience is temporary and that can give you an extraordinary appreciation for what you have today, as well as an acceptance of every outstanding imperfection in yourself and others. Things are due to change and that is okay. You can't always anticipate how life will surprise you or how things may work out even better than expected, but you know that hard times don't last.

19. USING "TEMPORARY" TO YOUR ADVANTAGE

"If you can dream—and not make dreams your master;
If you can think—and not make thoughts your aim;

If you can meet with Triumph and Disaster
And treat those two imposters just the same."

– Rudyard Kipling, "If"

The transient nature of life—everything, no matter how good or bad it is perceived to be, is only temporary.

Your life's journey will involve many uphills and downhills. Beyond awareness of the present moment is the valuable recognition of which one you are currently facing: a mountain at times, sure, but at other times, you'll find yourself on *easy street*. Don't miss these moments or periods in your life—it's true that they don't last forever. Our minds do seem to adjust to the familiar and ultimately, we take life for granted because of how normal and consistent it seems to be. Sometimes, happiness is not far away; instead, it is right where you are and you only need a gentle reminder. And yet, change is always on the horizon.

Consider what you love and appreciate most about your life today. It will not last forever, though your love for it might. Recognize this and you'll find yourself being more intentional about enjoying the company of a loved one, a close friend, times when you are healthy and feeling good, or time spent with your favorite hobby. It is all the more reason to immerse yourself in each moment, because you can't assume that things will be the same in the future.

Applying this philosophy to daily life can make even the greatest challenge seem surmountable. Even the worst-case scenario is something that is only temporary. This means that you can and will get through it, and if you can't, then you don't have to. For some, this is enough to relieve any anxiety about the future. It doesn't really matter what you will face; if you carry this philosophy with you, then you will already have the necessary self-belief to overcome. Willpower is easier to find when you understand that no challenge lasts forever. Ideally, this leads to a better appreciation of the times when life is good or easy. Whatever misfortune or struggle may lie in the future, it is not happening now and you can be grateful for that peace.

The thought of "finding" or "achieving" peace of

mind does make it seem like a destination, when in reality, it is an ongoing practice. It can be likened more to something you carry with you, or a temporary state that you visit from time to time. You can always find peace in the present moment if you look carefully. Happiness, joy, peace, or any other positive feeling you strive for, only exists in the moment when you appreciate the current but temporary "goodness" in your life. The opportunities you miss are the daily reflections on what is good in your life which may come and go. This is a natural part of being human since we experience tunnel vision while fixated on "what comes next."

Are you enjoying your journey? We are often so focused on setting and achieving goals, and getting *through* life that we forget to enjoy each moment along the way. And besides, life is likely to change between now and when you reach your goal—you simply can't control that. The value is found in what you learn along the way.

Just because "life is short" does not mean that you should rush through it. Many will say that they wish for peace and calm in their life, but they do not live that way. Slow down and let your time expand. Patience is worth developing, regardless of how others may act, because it allows you to be more intentional in your decision-making, in order to make the most of your time. When you slow down, you tend to think more clearly and deeply, helping you to make an informed decision. You create space to bask in the special moments in life instead of letting them pass you by; how often we forget how to just *take it easy*.

Making your own way means that you are taking ownership of your life and being intentional in the present while creating an exciting future with meaningful experiences and many possibilities. You can't do this when you are stuck and focused on the past.

Why do we love to romanticize the past? Because it feels so safe and certain since it is crystallized in our memory. But it wasn't that way at the time. We navigated the same amount of uncertainty then as we do now. Hard times came and went, we celebrated the good times, and the future ended up looking like our present. When we tell the story about how the past was better, we are doing ourselves a disservice by taking joy out of the present and hope out of the future.

Life is generally easier now than it has been in the past, but we find ourselves facing new and different challenges. Sometimes, we need to create hope and excitement in the form of a resting point in the future to get us through tough times. Why else would we agree to suffer, endure and overcome? Traditions ground us, allow us to celebrate life, and help us to mark the change and time that has passed. They afford the opportunity to set aside the daily hustle, and instead, reflect on what we have today. There is no greater celebration of what is good and temporary, yet you do not need to rely on holidays to create this type of appreciation in your daily life.

We will confront death in the last section of this book, but for now, we will use the idea of it to our advantage. The knowledge that your time is finite is an incredible gift which allows you to let go of anything unnecessary and unimportant. Otherwise, you will waste both your time and your life force which are very much temporary. Intentionality is incredibly key to making your own way—the recognition of what is temporary and the changes you are willing to make in your life as a result of that truth.

How many people before you came into this world and struggled to find their way, learned and improved, helped others, and then moved on? That's just how it goes. You can strive to better yourself and make the most of your time, as temporary as it may be, by finding balance in the process. Balance is the goal because balance is sustainable.

20. TOO SOFT, TOO HARD; JUST RIGHT

*"Nothing is so strong as gentleness.
Nothing is so gentle as real strength."*

– Ralph W. Sockman

Humans navigate a great deal of change to keep things in balance. The body and mind crave homeostasis and nature agrees—first conflict, then growth, and finally balance.

Earlier, in "Enough," you probably considered the main question: Are you someone who needs to loosen up or tighten up? Hopefully, by this point in the book, you have picked up a better awareness of your nature. You have an idea of who you are and what you want to work on in a general sense. Understand that your biggest strength is also usually your most notable weakness.

For example, anxiety can push you to do great things. You don't want to let it push you too far—there needs to be space to experience all emotions—but it can drive you to be successful by ensuring that you are doing "enough." People who suffer significant trauma or setbacks often work incredibly hard to prove themselves and they accomplish a great deal, but they may never feel that they are "enough." *That* is why we must find balance.

Balance is built on self-awareness. It's not about being perfect, it's about accepting your struggles and learning how to compensate for them in a healthy way. So, *what* if you feel like you're too lazy or uptight in general? Laugh at yourself and loosen up, or try a bit harder if you need to, but by all means, you'll never need to be perfect. You likely bring many other great qualities that balance out your family or group of friends; pay attention to those instead. Our world cannot exist in balance without every different, unique thing that you and everyone you know brings to the table.

How do you want your own balance to feel?

Balance is something we create within ourselves. Yes, our experiences will affect and shape us, but we are ultimately responsible for how we show up in the world. Consider this:

It's normal to expect that our happiness will be helped by many things— good food, rest, exercise, friends and family, our favorite hobbies— but we often make the mistake of blaming those same things for our unhappiness without asking: Am I bringing a positive attitude to the table? Am I generating happiness and joy from myself? It is not enough to rely on externals alone for your happiness. If you want to be happier and more laid back in life, no one is going to do that for you.

Positivity takes effort— it is a recognition and subsequent defiance of life's challenges and tragedies. Gratitude takes perspective— it is an awareness of those less fortunate than you. You won't (and you really shouldn't) be happy or positive all the time, but the idea is that if you put some effort into how you act and behave, then it will affect your mood. Again, the rusty wheel analogy: at first you might find yourself in a funk, but once you start to shake it off, laugh, feel better, and try to be a bit more hopeful, things start flowing again.

Don't aim to change the world to your liking. Instead, change yourself, then see if the world is already the way you want it to be.

Make no mistake; a gentle spirit is invaluable in a tough world, but cultivating some form of inner toughness is a necessity. Willpower is the only consistent way to get from where you are to where you want to be. Other things may come and go as we face life's challenges, losing and finding our balance again and again. Expect that you will lose your balance at some point, and that is okay. Humans are both incredibly resilient and shockingly fragile at the same time. Our physical, mental, emotional and spiritual states all seem to feed each other in an upward, or downward, spiral. Find ways to be gentle with yourself when it's time to rebuild your strength. Then, invoke a defiant attitude in the face of adversity. The right combination of stress and calm can be rewarding, even rejuvenating, if not pushed too far.

Things can go wrong in life—sometimes horribly wrong—but if you survive what happens, you will find your balance again and keep moving forward. This is strength of heart. It will benefit you to have the right combination of resilience and lightheartedness in your journey even when things go wrong. Seriousness can develop into a disease that weighs you down and with too much pain and seriousness together, you create anger.

Like a fire that cannot be controlled, holding anger inside will damage you and then those around you. And while it may work well as fuel for a time, you will eventually burn out. Anger is a valid emotion, but it is often a sign that we have pain or fear hidden just below the surface. It signals that we feel a perceived slight or unfairness in life, but life is often unfair by our standards so we must choose instead to make ourselves better.

The balance you choose to carry will affect your daily experience of life. It impacts your self-image, your relationships, and how you make meaning from your experiences. Can you balance ambition with gratitude? Can you forge yourself into someone who is strong but gentle, firm but understanding, driven but lighthearted, focused but relaxed? The relationship between your internal and external states is mutual— you can influence but not control external events. Similarly, external events can influence but not control the balance that lives in you.

21. THE MIND IS A MIRROR

"Whatever we plant in our subconscious mind and nourish with repetition and emotion will one day become a reality."

— Earl Nightingale

How do you live with vulnerability in a world that offers way too much information about what could go wrong?

Consciousness is a precious gift. Your entire world is a projection that your mind and senses allow you to experience. It is crucial to pay attention to how we feed this projection based on the input we provide.

Spending too much time on the negative events in the

world can reduce hope and increase feelings of helplessness, like bad ingredients in the recipe of your mind. All the while, your own future remains undetermined. Be careful with the "ingredients" that you put into this recipe because they influence your thoughts, feelings and perception of reality. What you focus on grows in your attention.

It's understandable that our minds are more likely to get stuck on the negative rather than the positive, but what is most interesting is how you can focus on one idea or theme and it will continue to show up in your world. This isn't coincidence. It is our subconscious ability to train our mind's attention to find evidence for certain ideas or beliefs. This is why it is so important to be careful about the information and media that you consume. It affects your perception of reality in ways that you cannot possibly control. Consume paranoia and guess what you will begin to feel? Paranoid!

Information is like food—it bloats you when you consume too much. The mind has to compensate for more and more uncertainty that may have no realistic impact on your life. It is an individual responsibility to manage the amount that you consume. Too much of it makes it hard for you to think rationally; too little of it makes it hard for you to learn and grow.

It is *very* difficult to look away from the circus show of politics, worst-case scenarios, and bad things happening around the world, but you must if you want to live a normal life… if you want to live your life.

It has *always* been this way. First, they capture your

attention and then they capture your emotion. We are social, emotional creatures and it only becomes harder to look away once emotionally invested. Emotion leads to action and not always the good kind. The more media you consume, the more you feel you *have to* consume. Your opinion is no longer your own but one you adopted through emotion. It is a profound distraction from what you find uninteresting or unexciting about your own life. And then the subconscious mind begins to assume that what is happening out in the world is actually happening in *your* individual world. It's not.

Awareness of what others are going through in life is incredibly important. That does not mean you should continually consume information about negative things going on in the world; how much of it is actionable on your part? There is no path to meaning in your own life through events that are so far outside of your control. It's not fair to your mind to provide a steady influx of information that makes you feel powerless. That feeling will lower the likelihood that you take action in the first place. Remember: influence, not control. You only have so much energy to commit towards improving your life and staying on track for your specific goals. If you care about improving the world and reducing its suffering, you will do that through your work, societal contributions and through selflessness, which we will explore in the next section of this book.

There is a great deal of information available about how the world is a "bad" or "dangerous" place. It is impossible to say that the world is a wholly "good" place, but the reality is too complex to make a complete assessment. What is true, however, is that every creature in nature is motivated strongly by both love and fear. And love seems to exist as the connective tissue. Somehow, we manage to forget that as we get older.

Children face the world with excitement, imagination and curiosity, but adults become unhappy when they give these up to fit in with the society that is already in place. You are born into this world as a blank slate, but then distorted by the issues carried forward from past generations. It is then your responsibility to grow from these issues and become better. As you grow up, you are told who you will be. See if you can unravel that and decide for yourself who you really are.

And if something bad does happen in your life? It does *not* make you a bad person. In no way is it a reflection of who you are and it is no more meaningful than just "something that happened" to you. In the early chapters of this book, we discussed the idea of overcoming challenges and training your mind to help you solve real problems in life, rather than getting fixated on problems outside of your control. Bad things will happen and you can try to respond positively, but life happens to everyone.

Maybe you can relate to a common story; you form beliefs as you grow into adulthood. This framework makes sense, until you see or experience something that strongly disagrees with your understanding of the world. Some will retreat into their old beliefs, seeking comfort from uncertainty. This causes inner conflict because the mind now has evidence of the contrary. We must slowly and regularly update our understanding of the world.

Help your mind by providing the necessary input and perspective. Remind yourself of what you love about life so that the mind does not so easily forget. Refresh your perspective: others are less fortunate than you, others are in worse health than you, others do not have your relationships, work, and safety... the list goes on. Help your mind to see a more accurate reflection of reality.

Ultimately, you get the final say on who you see in the mirror. What do you see in yourself? What are your strengths and weaknesses? Self-belief is possibly the most important trait that is reflected into your world. What do you think happens if you give yourself that before any challenge and watch as you face your fears?

Imagine yourself to be like any other part of nature—a plant or an animal. How does *anything* in nature respond to love and nurturing? It grows in a healthy way. Self-belief and joy are exactly that; they are intangible forces of strength that lead to improved happiness and resilience. Joy is something you cultivate within and it exists for everyone, almost without trying. True freedom happens when your happiness is not dependent on anything external. The joy inside you is then mirrored in your health and your outer world through your interactions.

Focus on what you put *into* this world—physically, mentally, financially, or otherwise—and you will be surprised by the myriad ways these efforts return to you and others. Just as it was in the chapter "Enough," it's important to give yourself regular reminders about what you are putting into your life—good food, exercise, work, taking care of others, exciting plans for the future. It can be anything, but it helps your mind to stay focused on the good in your life. Those who cannot recognize "enough" good in their life will get lost in the never-ending search for "more."

22. WHEN HEDONISM REIGNS

"I feel like there is always something trying to pull us back into sleep, that there is this sort of seductive quality in all the hedonistic pleasures that pull on us."

– bell hooks

The devil on your shoulder, the monster inside... the dark side of human nature carries many names, but we know that it exists in all of us and manifests in various ways. This does not make any person "bad" at their core; it is a normal part of being human that we will make mistakes out of fear or anger. Growth is acknowledging this part of you, whatever it may be, and creating a self-awareness of its presence—temptation, greed, entitlement, selfish desire, manipulation and more. These impulses are driven by our animal nature and we must do what we can to know and accept our imperfections. It becomes even more difficult when something bad happens to you. You may believe that it is your fault, that you deserved it, or that you should have prevented it from happening—this is the mind trying to create meaning behind a painful experience as to *why* it might have happened.

Sadly, it is often in our nature to ignore our successes while internalizing responsibility for bad things that just *happen*. Then, guilt. You may mistakenly believe that you deserve more suffering. This can happen individually or on a much larger scale when self-defeat leads to more bad decisions. It is a dangerous cycle.

As social creatures, each of us has a responsibility not to hurt ourselves or others, and further feed the pain of this world.

Sure signs of moral decay are antisocial behaviors that indicate the following attitudes: "Why should I care?" or "Nothing matters" or "Everyone dies in the end, anyway." Unfortunately, those attitudes would only make sense in containment where one person's life does not affect anyone else's. And that's just not our reality. Recall the many dysregulated lizard brains and monkey minds; if left unresolved, humans will carry pain with them and transfer it to others. People go to great lengths, even hurting themselves and others in an attempt to find peace and happiness.

Yes, happiness is important in life, but you must be mindful about sacrificing long-term fulfillment in exchange for short-term pleasure. And you can do your best not to let your decisions negatively impact others in the process. When you put your needs in front of others, somehow, you end up as the one who suffers. Our souls carry the weight of our misdeeds, our spirits feel the impact of moral injury, and our lives are entangled in ways we cannot see.

We can find our way out of the darkness and out of the cycle of pain. "Comparison is the thief of joy" is a common saying that misses the mark because it assumes that all comparison is with those who have a better life than you. This is an incredibly helpful and necessary exercise. Your life is one of eight *billion* on this planet and that number grows much larger when you consider every other conscious living being, as well. Regularly recognizing others' struggles will lead to more appreciation of your own life. You can relieve your own suffering through the recognition of the suffering of others and there is always guaranteed to be someone who is worse off than you. We step out of pain and find our way back to compassion.

Perspective and humility can save you from the greatest despair. How much life do you need to live, how much do you need to experience for yourself? At some point, you might take an honest step back from your life and let out a deep sigh, only to realize that your life has indeed already been "enough" compared to others.

And still, we often seek out "more" in an attempt to find something that we feel is missing. It seems like it should be simple, but it can be quite difficult to fully understand what fulfills you. Taking time to answer this question might help you to avoid a lot of unnecessary searching. Pure happiness may not be what is really missing in your life, but it may be feelings of capability, peace, acceptance and purpose that you are after.

Life is not meant to be constantly exciting, stimulating, and busy—this is deception on the part of modern society. Boredom is the cousin of peace. Paradoxically, the *more* we have in our lives, the *less* we value what is actually in our lives. The mind can adjust to virtually any standard of living. If you feel that you don't have "enough" in your life, and you can't define what is actually "enough" for you, the mind will just continue pushing the idea that you need more. It will continue creating problems even when there are none. This automatic process can only be interrupted by you and you alone.

For just a moment, if you let go of every narrative in your mind—every worry or concern about the past or future—and allow your mind to be clear and open, you'll find that your true nature is to be calm and joyful in the present. When you find yourself fully present, you may realize that there was nothing else that you were necessarily seeking besides the ability to experience life fully. You find happiness by wanting what you already have, when you *feel* that your life is enough. But what a joy it is to keep living.

Maybe you continue living life in the same way that you have in the past, but eventually, you reach a point where you seem to find it less fulfilling. If you are lucky, you will realize that you have solved the foundational problems in your life and at that time, it may feel more meaningful to go out and solve problems for others rather than to continue looking for ways to improve your own life. This is not to say that you shouldn't enjoy your life and make the most of it.

You aren't meant to experience only yourself—you are meant to experience life around you. If your driving force is limited to your own life, which will come and go as part of something much bigger, you may find yourself feeling empty. Expanding your purpose to everyone and everything else around you will unlock a higher level of joy and fulfillment.

23. SOMETHING BIGGER, SOMETHING MORE

"The smallest seed of faith is better than the largest fruit of happiness."

– Henry David Thoreau

No one can tell you what to believe, but faith in *anything* larger than yourself connects you to something bigger and leads to a universal strength that anyone can experience.

In our quest for knowledge, we often forget that we cannot know everything. Some part of life will always remain a mystery and we must find acceptance of that. The magic lies not in our ability to understand and solve problems, but in a humble embrace of the unknown. Science and faith can coexist in the same way that there is truly an art and a science to living. Interestingly, faith seems to be inversely correlated with personal control and that tells us a lot about our nature—we have an inherent psychological tendency to take both the good and bad things that happen to us as our responsibility or our *fault*. The more "in control" we feel over our life, the less likely we are to turn to something larger than ourselves. The less control we feel, the more likely we are to put our faith in something larger, something *else* that might have control.

Desiring to feel safe, accepted and valued is a natural human ambition. It is beautiful to share beliefs with a community. But your individual responsibility is to consider things on your own, as well. What does life mean to you?

Technically speaking, it is just as illogical to believe in "nothing" as it is to believe in "something"—both assume a correct and final assessment of reality. We will truly never know, so it is your right to believe as you wish. Belief is the art and logic is the science of life.

Whether you believe in God, gods, nature, the universe, or none of these, the important thing is to understand that everything in our world is ultimately connected through the same life force. We are made of the same *stuff*. We exist in relation to many who came before us and many who will come after us; we rely on those who create and provide what we enjoy, and we sustain ourselves through what we consume, which comes from this place. Carrying this mindset and belief will allow you to see your connection and purpose as it relates to everyone else around you. It affects how you cooperate, find common ground with your neighbors, and endeavor to help those in need.

When people practice religion, for example, they are cultivating a sense of love, joy and connectivity for themselves, their loved ones and a higher purpose. There is a release through letting go of personal attachment to become part of something larger. This is real action on the part of the individual or community and it can make the world a better place if applied in that way. When we loosen our attachment to ourselves, we find space to value others that much more.

What you see as being larger than you can be anything: friends, family, your work, your community, or your religion. By function of living in this world, you will always be part of something larger than yourself. And what you add to this world will affect your ecosystem in small and large ways.

This is the antidote to loneliness—the recognition that you are never really alone; not in your beliefs, actions, experiences, existence, and connection to this present reality which you share with many others.

The ripple effect of your actions will affect your children, your community and even future generations. Even small decisions seem to find their way down the line—how you treat your physical, mental, financial health and more. What begins as insignificant becomes valuable in the grand scheme of life. You can take pride in knowing that your efforts, the good you put *in*, really does matter in the big picture, and you can fall back on that one truth—that you are never really alone.

What an amazing relief it is to learn that "life is not

about me." It's hard to imagine a greater gift. Some people will go their whole life without realizing this gift. Instead, carrying the weight of misunderstanding and the thought that life depends on them alone—the pressure, stress, and fear you might experience when you *feel* alone. Only when you take a step back can you realize that "life will be okay." Always remember that you are one tree in a much larger forest.

Sometimes, it is not enough to get motivated for yourself alone, but you can find new strength when you consider what you are willing to do for others. Fulfillment is found in your ability to transcend yourself—to walk past your own ego and not be enslaved by its demands; to feel like a hero for yourself and those around you. Then, you will know what it means to be free, self-assured, and confident with your place in this world.

This book began with taking responsibility for your life; now it continues with finding the strength to help others.

24. LOST AT THE MOUNTAINTOP

"What we do for ourselves dies with us. What we do for others and the world remains and is immortal."

– Albert Pike

While there remains a great deal of suffering around the world, why is it that people with good lives (by most objective standards) are still unhappy and unfulfilled? Surely, as you continue to invest in your own life, it should only get better... right?

Remember how, if left unregulated, the mind will continually seek out new problems to solve? The good news is that many people exist with no substantial, foundational problems in their lives; at least not the ones keeping them in survival mode. Many people have enough food, safety, shelter, and financial resources. Beyond that, people have access to a great deal of entertainment and technology to enhance their life. Loneliness is a widespread issue, but social interaction is more possible and accessible than ever. So, what's missing? How is it possible that people can have so much, yet still feel an aching emptiness in their life?

Somewhere along the way, we probably forgot what it really means to be human. Beyond your individual foundation and security, we discussed the importance of healthy relationships and the value of your work, as well as the joys of spending your free time with a sense of individuality. Finding success in these foundational and relational needs can help you to live in a consistent, enjoyable routine. But we need to go a step further. We must find a way to fully satisfy both the animal *and* the human in your nature. Along with reflection and making meaning from your experiences, fulfillment is found in the following:

1. Belonging: Intimate connections where you are valued for who you are.
2. Honor: Esteem developed through achievement and service to others.
3. Purpose: The ability to realize your full potential.

The best part? There is an intersection where these three meet—that is your unique place in the world.

If you want to be rich, work to serve yourself. If you want to be happy and fulfilled, work to serve others. And yes, it is possible to do both. Get creative! Through your work, valued relationships, and your purpose; can you combine what you like to do with what you do well? And can you do so in a way that generally helps others and adds to the world, rather than taking from others to add to your life? Remember that your efforts, big and small, help to keep the world moving forward. This section of the book is about moving forward while not leaving others behind.

With diminishing returns on your happiness alone, you will reach a position when you know that your own life cannot necessarily get better. If you get to this stage, you have a fortunate opportunity.

By this point in the book, you likely have a better understanding of yourself and what you value. Hopefully, you feel the urgency to embrace your life and individuality. And now you can understand your responsibility as a caring creature and as part of something bigger than yourself. Throughout your life, it will help you to situate yourself among everyone else who is also on their own journey. Consider these two perspectives from the same situation:

1) Think of what you are missing in your life → Feel envy or anxiety → Harder to notice the goodness in your life

Compared to:

2) Think of others who have less than you → Feel gratitude → Easier to let go of fear and sadness, and instead, appreciate your life → Become motivated to seek out those who need help

The first creates a never-ending loop. You will always feel the need for more and you may never know enough, in that case. Your animal nature may never be satiated and it will be hard to know peace. But that is not your entire nature as a human being. You can find "enough" for yourself, and then consider the perspective of others.

The second is reality. In this scenario, you can find acceptance, belonging, purpose, self-assurance and inner peace. You can go beyond yourself to provide for others by understanding their struggles and caring for their needs.

You can't alleviate your own suffering by focusing on yourself more and more. At some point, you have to focus on others and what they might be going through.

If you ignore the pain in the world, you miss an opportunity to find purpose and fulfillment through service to others. When you consume media about the negativity in the world without taking action, you will feel negative and powerless. When you seek out real suffering in your community and the world, you suddenly become very capable. This is a subtle distinction—you can reduce the pain of the world without internalizing it. Just as you wouldn't take pleasure in someone else's pain, you shouldn't take pain from their pain, either. Allow it to inspire gratitude for your own life as well as the motivation to make a difference. If your foundational and relational needs are met, you are in a perfect situation to transcend yourself and fulfill your greatest human potential.

True divinity is reaching the top of the mountain, then turning around to help others find their way up.

25. THE CARING CREATURE

*"I slept and dreamt that life was joy.
I awoke and saw that life was service.
I acted and behold, service was joy."*

– Rabindranath Tagore

The world has always been a dark place, but humans create their own light. From caring for our own offspring to helping complete strangers, we have a natural inclination to help others. Maybe it's just the way we are engineered; we are likely to feel our best when we care about ideas and other people more than we care about ourselves. Life is meant to be an outward experience in that way. After you develop the necessary safety and security within yourself, you go on to expand your world.

The world is not intent on hurting you. Life does not

wish to see you suffer. Life *does* wish for you to find meaningful stress and, through that, meaningful growth. Even if you have been hurt in life, regardless of whether or not it was your fault, you have a responsibility to yourself to move forward. If you can heal yourself with the necessary compassion, then you will realize your ability to heal others, too.

For the world to change for the better, it has to start with compassion. For you to change for the better, it also starts with compassion. Compassion comes from a place of strength and selflessness—the willingness to drop what you are doing and focus on what someone else is going through. It also means that you are able to accept and support yourself through tough times. Whether it is for yourself or for others, it takes strength to turn *towards*, rather than to turn away. Like any form of strength, you might find yourself fatigued if you are constantly helping others with their needs. Remember that balance is what is sustainable; care for yourself, then care for others.

There is a particular joy you feel when you put a smile on someone else's face, when you remind them of why they matter, or if you help them when they are at their lowest point.

You will surprise many people when you treat them with compassion and kindness. Why is the world this way? Why is that basic human dignities are unexpected? We let too many distractions get in the way of our true nature. Some people have little choice—due to their circumstances they are forced into finding ways to meet their survival needs, sometimes at the expense of others—but for everyone else, what is the excuse?

By our nature, we have an obligation to do right by others. We must find it in ourselves to care.

Humans are intrinsically motivated to care for others. You are wired to be social and helpful. It's built into your DNA. A life built around serving your own interests will always be missing one final piece; a part of your nature left unsatisfied. Kindness and compassion towards others boost our own feelings of well-being. There is a yearning to find agreement, compromise, and belonging with our connections which serve us as much as they serve others.

There is no logical reason for this form of altruism—that doing right by someone else also benefits your spirit. Maybe once upon a time we would have been motivated to cooperate for our survival, yet it feels great to give even when you get nothing in return, just to see that someone else has enough. Fear, greed, and selfishness would tell you to take more for yourself, to make sure you have enough, and to forget your worry for others. The animal, the lizard or the monkey, would tell you to defend your own and distrust others. When you act on those impulses, you continue to feel those feelings. This is a great paradox of the human condition—you take more happiness for yourself by giving to others. Go beyond your animal impulses and you will find the purity of the human spirit.

It's true that you are the only person responsible for your own happiness. But when you see someone else who is down, you can't help but care, right? It's reciprocal. Have no doubt that there are others who think of you now and also wish for you to be happy. The fears, concerns and insecurities that fuel the desire for self-improvement; they exist *because* you care for yourself. And that care and compassion extends to everyone else who shares your same experience of struggle, pain, uncertainty, life and death.

Many, many people will never know what it means to have enough resources to support themselves and their family. Fortunately, many people will also have more than enough and likely more than they could ever need in their lifetime. Compared to what you give to others, your soul is paid back with something much bigger—true joy, fulfillment, and inner peace. These are the prized feelings that most people spend their entire lives searching for, without considering what they are really seeking. Real, genuine pride comes from the ability to care and provide for others.

26. HOW TO FEED YOUR EGO (THE RIGHT WAY)

"The ultimate aim of the ego is not to see something, but to be something."

– Muhammad Iqbal

What stops you from moving past your own worries and self-concerns? Is it fear you might be judged, discarded, or otherwise left behind? Are you driven by a need to prove yourself?

Maybe you fear that if you don't worry for yourself, *who will?*

And yet, when you go beyond yourself and leave a self-centered worldview behind, it feels *right*. It may seem like a counterintuitive process but transcending the fears, worries and desires of the ego also means transcending entitlement, insecurity, and self-preservation. It means you have firmly decided that as a human, you are "enough."

This is the same as developing unconditional love and acceptance for yourself. It is normal to get fixated on your past mistakes, or expect that you might not be good enough in the future, but at the end of the day, these are just ideas that exist in your mind alone. They have as much power as you feed them and we must be responsible for how we feed our own pain.

The unhealthy ego can never know what it is to be "enough" in this world. More money, possessions, attention, accomplishments, validation, and climbing through societal ranks… Judging yourself on how successful you appear based on standards put in place by others, rather than your own… Feeling good about yourself only when someone *else* decides you are "enough"… This is the opposite of true belonging where you are accepted when you show up as the person that you really are. And it will never, ever heal the ache you feel inside that says, "*I am not good enough.*"

The worst feeling in the world is to worry about your "self." Not because it is selfish— in fact, it's the most natural thing we all do—but because you know that you would much rather be worried about everyone and everything else. You would hear what your partner or best friend said, you would really sink in and do your best work, you would fully enjoy your favorite activity, or you would just be comfortable to relax and do nothing.

Only you have the power to give yourself that compassion and freedom. See if you can't let go of these illusions that you are somehow not good enough.

At the beginning of this book, we laid out a foundation for good physical and mental health. We also discussed the idea of moving past your most basic survival instincts. Ego will drive us to seek many things to "find" our peace and happiness, but we can transcend these urges to become something much greater. The person who tries to conquer the world finds themself in a fight with envy, greed, anger, frustration, and denial. The person who conquers themself instead, finds peace, self-assurance, clarity, and insight. Humans, at their highest level of being, are truly amazing creatures who are capable of creating their own inner peace and acceptance.

It takes courage for a social animal to be true to themself but you will find new power through acceptance and self-belief. A healthy ego is a sign of a person who values their place in the world, while seeing themselves as "enough." Focus on what drives you towards your purpose in life. It is about using your individuality to do good for yourself and others.

You can judge yourself based on the efforts you put in, the way you treat others, and what you give back to this world instead of what happens to you, what others think, and the ways that life seems unfair. Failures in life are inevitable but your character is not comprised of your failures and mistakes. No person is perfect. What if you paid more attention to the positive influence you have already had?

Imagine that you reach the end of your life—this is

the end of the road and you are ready to pass on. Before you go, you turn and feel a sense of awe in what you see:

Behind you, spreading out over a great distance, stands every living being that you impacted in your life— family, friends, coworkers, pets, strangers. Everyone is there to see you off and thank you for the simple gestures that you thought went unnoticed— each small kindness that touched others, the times you helped someone when they were close to giving up and you didn't know… every bit of effort.

There is living proof of your selflessness in others; the ripple effect of your existence. The ego can see this and finally rest, knowing for certain that you are "enough."

It is intimidating, but necessary, to ask yourself the big questions: Who are you? What do you value and what will you give back to life? What brings you the feeling of honor? The only real answer is the one you hear from your inner voice, without the influence of anyone else around you.

27. HONOR

"When the will defies fear, when duty throws the gauntlet down to fate, when honor scorns to compromise with death—that is heroism."

– Robert G. Ingersoll

Think of a hero in your life. What do you admire about them? It could be many things: their selflessness, their willingness to keep going, the way they take action despite their fear, or their commitment to doing what is right and what is necessary. You can embody this everyday hero, too, in all of your intentions and decisions. There will always be people who need help, not only in the form of your unique gifts and talents, but also in small acts of compassion and understanding. Your selflessness can become a form of daily greatness.

You can't save the world, but you *can* contribute to the goodness in it.

Honor in oneself and one's actions is enough to stifle even the most insecure ego. It is enough to remove self-doubt and replace it with self-assurance. You can maintain a sense of humility and confidence—no one is better than you and no one is worse than you. If you approach each person you meet with this equal respect, they will feel it and notice it. You garner esteem from others not only by how you treat them but by how you treat yourself. Regardless of how others act, you can confront them with kindness and generosity. That takes a great deal of strength; it means that you are confident, self-assured and you care more about how you act or react than how others behave. It means that you don't take things personally. When you set an example for others, they might reflect on their own shortcomings and see how it is possible to carry oneself in a better way.

One of the most important decisions in life is determining "how" you want to be. How do you want to face life? Similar to the previous ideas presented on finding balance, how you carry yourself will affect how you experience life. It will affect how you see yourself. And it will determine how quickly you can find yourself and bounce back from difficult moments in life.

Everyone makes mistakes, has imperfections, and has regrets. We make the best decisions possible with the information available. Then, we have the ability to recognize our wrongdoing, commit to improvement and go beyond where we are now. Redemption is found not in shaming yourself, but in honorable acts that improve yourself, serve others, and benefit the world.

Compassion and integrity go hand in hand, both for ourselves and others. Your intuition usually knows the next "right" thing to do. When you honor others and you act selflessly, somehow, you are often the one who is paid back. Do the right thing just for the sake of it and not for any external reward or reason. Then, you will find that the reward becomes internal.

When you find balance, act with honor, find belonging in your relationships, understand yourself and what you are able to contribute to the world, your purpose in life begins to take shape.

Purpose happens when you create the path in front of you, then take it; you make your own way. Clarity comes naturally when you follow your intuition about what is meaningful to you, uncovering which talents you can offer the world and what values you wish to uphold. No one can give your purpose to you— it is an ongoing feeling that occurs when you align intentional decision-making with your values.

Your purpose may be unique to you, but there are some things we all share in common. All people wish to meet their basic needs, then create goals for their life, all while maintaining a sense of spirituality and connection.

Consider the moral arc for humanity: once we surpass survival needs, we are able to build incredible lives for ourselves. Once we have incredible lives with impactful work and meaningful connections, we can proceed to help others by alleviating their suffering. What a beautiful path.

Rise, and stand tall in the face of your fate with the knowledge that you have led a good, full life where you sought to help others—a life led with honor and dedication. Is there a greater reward than experiencing life with a sense of inner peace?

In the end, given the rarity of your existence, it is simply a great honor to be alive.

28. RELAX, YOU'VE DONE THIS BEFORE

"Each thing is of like form from everlasting and comes round again in its cycle."

– Marcus Aurelius

Many readers will skip right to these last few chapters because humans will always be curious about death. Try to keep that same attitude as you read— replacing any fear with a sense of curiosity about "the end."

Death can be a challenging topic to explore, but it is worth meeting it head-on. On one hand, it feels like the great unknown; on the other hand, there is comfort in the certainty and inevitability of it. Curiosity is a helpful attitude when you approach anything unknown. The more you face it, the less you fear it. One of the best things about being your own person is that you can form your own opinions on anything; you don't have to accept the opinions given to you. In this case, you can consider your relationship with death and what it means to you.

As you get older, you replace ignorance with acceptance. It's true that death is ever present and it can be uncomfortable to recognize your own vulnerability and mortality. Look around in nature and you'll see that no animal is guaranteed the next day. Again, this can be reassuring in a way because of how it connects us all, but difficult to fully grasp nonetheless. Some may find themselves stressed, frustrated, or even despairing about their own existence. But remember, the alternative is never having existed in the first place.

The value of the present moment has been highlighted throughout this book and in this final section, it becomes only more valuable. Remember, there is no running from what you experience in the present. That truth alone can solve most of your anxieties or worries about what *might* happen. Having an attitude of acceptance, the willpower to face and overcome challenges, and a sense of gratitude and belonging as part of something much bigger. These are what will serve you as you embrace your life's journey.

What would hurt more, your own passing or the loss of someone you love? The irony of your passing is that you are the only person whose experience in life won't be affected by it, whereas others may mourn you or miss you while they are here.

Losing a loved one is a profoundly difficult experience, but what's the worst that can happen to *you*? Pain—

you've felt that before. Losing consciousness— you already spend time asleep. Beyond that, there is nothing to really fear if your own fear is the worst you can actually experience.

Can death be considered a "bad" thing in any sense? The circumstances around it can be painful, the loss we feel from our attachment is natural, and the perceived future that is no longer there. It is imagined and we may grieve that, too. But death itself is part of change and nature, like everything else we do in life. Through the life passed down to you from your ancestors, your inherited genes connect you to the many iterations of existence that pieces of you have already endured. Death and nature connect us all.

And if not for any social taboo often surrounding it, death would just be considered a normal part of nature. While some cultures choose to avoid the topic completely, others celebrate death for its meaning and significance. It represents the peaceful rest after one's journey through life.

An interesting paradox is that the happiest and most comfortable people really accept and even embrace the thought of death. But they love life, and they would not want to lose it, right? With full acceptance, these people are able to live their life fully and freely, with nothing holding them back. Developing a comfort with your own mortality is a great investment in the enjoyment of your life. Denial will cause an underlying anxiety that is impossible to avoid. For that same reason, you should fear the avoidance of life more than your eventual death.

You cannot allow the fear of physical death to limit

the life of your spirit. Acceptance and mental preparation for death will allow you to free up energy for the greater pursuits in your life. When you are busy living in the fullness of your own life while recognizing that many others will have a more difficult journey than your own, the prospect of death does not seem so ultimately bad—this is the cool wave of acceptance. The goal is to strike a balance between enjoying and desiring more life, while having gratitude for all the good that you've already enjoyed.

You don't have to deny the inevitable unknown, you can face it like anything else in life. Our ability to consider our own death and how it relates to our life is a unique gift. Imagine yourself on your deathbed now. Do you have any regrets about your life? Is there any way that you would have lived differently? And can you take those ideas and apply them now, changing the course of your life beginning with today?

If you can visualize your own funeral, and therefore all of your connections to loved ones, you can see the temporary but powerful force of your own life.

29. BORROWED TIME

"Because I could not stop for Death –
He kindly stopped for me –

The Carriage held but just ourselves –
And Immortality."

– Emily Dickinson, "Because I could not stop for Death"

For a brief time your consciousness awakens, and then what?

Confront the idea of death and you'll begin to understand what kind of relationship you have with the unknown. More importantly, it's an indicator of your ability to accept uncertainty at the highest level. How much is your focus on what is out of your control, including the experience of death, versus everything that is still in your control while you are alive? Does it feel better to think about death or simply ignore it? Most will say, "Life is short," and go about their life as they normally would because it is certainly outside of anyone's control, but not outside the influence created through how they live. For others, considering our brief lifespan is a worthwhile and meaningful exercise.

You should not have to live with a fear of death (remember, life and death connect you to everyone and everything else), but it is useful to consider it when deciding what is most important in life. Everything—relationships, hobbies, happiness and time—becomes more valuable when considered against it. Intentionality has been highlighted as key to making your own way in life; what is more intentional than considering how to use your limited time? The impulse of death can strengthen you to take action and make necessary changes in your life. We are a species that endures and overcomes.

Humanity has faced many setbacks and challenges throughout history, but it hasn't stopped us. Like a growing plant that meets concrete, we keep growing through. Nature and life always seem to find a way. Your journey is part of that much larger story and while you cannot know the future, you can embrace your path and your fate. There is a good chance it is longer and more enjoyable than many others out there.

There are reminders of our mortality everywhere. Subtle reminders which bring gratitude and appreciation for the life you have today. What happens to someone else may not impact your life in any direct way, but it still serves as a reminder that we live on borrowed time. The double-edged sword of living a good life is that there is just more at stake. You feel more attachment to all that you love and live for. Allow that to fill you with appreciation and selflessness rather than fear and selfishness. The ego may stress the importance of your own life, the feeling that the weight of the world is on your shoulders, and the thought that you are alone in anything. It couldn't be further from reality.

Try to imagine eight billion other humans, just like you, wandering this planet at the same moment. It's nearly impossible to fully comprehend and yet you can consider our world the same way we see ants or fish or birds or any other part of nature, simply acting within our nature. There is a weightless feeling that comes with the recognition of how small we really are. And yet, we are mighty in our ability to think creatively and live meaningful lives. You can live and act outside your structures, you can break inherent patterns when they are unhelpful, you can live with an awareness of your ego and animal nature.

Life is a wonderful and temporary gift. You have the opportunity to find special relationships, engaging work, and unique hobbies. You can *enjoy* life while helping others and trying to avoid creating more pain. You can create an inner peace that you will one day leave behind for your loved ones and the future of the world when your time has passed. Every small effort and kindness that impacts the lives of others is what reverberates throughout time.

Can you look inside and recognize that you are a good person and you have had a good life? The point is to live fully so that you feel no regret when your time comes to an end.

You exist through the life force of many who have passed already; through those who saw the world with eyes not unlike your own. So much had to happen for you to exist at all and there will be a great deal of time after you, too, but this is your time—now. This is a calling to live with great intention.

What do you need to live a full and meaningful life? Which regrets can you accept; which can you not? You can't change life, but you can choose to make the absolute most of it. No one is bigger than death, but anyone can be larger than life because you decide the quality, not the quantity, of how you experience life.

We come into this world, we enjoy our time under the sun, and then we make way for new life.

30. THE OPPOSITE OF LONELY

"Each departed friend is a magnet that attracts us to the next world."

– Jean Paul

We do this together.

By now, you can feel how everything discussed in this book is connected: the body, the mind, your relationship to yourself and others, your environment, your work and impact on the world, your purpose, your children, your spirituality and even death.

Resisting death is resisting change, which we cannot do; for it is in our nature. Born first into the world as only a body, you form connections throughout your lifetime as you grow the fullness of your spirit, only to help others continue on. Just as leaves fall from trees to fertilize soil for the sapling to rise, human life rises and falls as the earth inhales then exhales new life.

The cycle of birth into life, into death, and rebirth into new life again occurs across the universe on a scale much larger than we can comprehend. We can never separate ourselves from nature and the mystery of the unknown. One thing is certain, however: you don't know what form your energy will go on to become after your life. At least, you haven't experienced it yet.

You can combat existential dread with existential joy—knowing the likelihood of existing in the first place is unbelievably slim. How lucky are you to exist at the same time as so many amazing people and so many amazing things? How comforting to know that there are people out there right now who truly love you? Some of them you may not have even met yet, but you will.

Suffering, loss and death may very well be the price we pay for time with the things we enjoy and the people we love. And even when someone passes, their energy and impact remains in this place. Think of all the great people—survivors, adventurers and creators—who came and went before you. When your time comes, you'll be ready too, and it will be okay.

Life is a process of letting go.

The longer you live, the more you realize that life was never about being perfect or getting everything you want. It was always just an opportunity to try, fail, and learn while doing your best—a chance to see what you can give back, share, and enjoy with others, and a moment in time to make your own way.

Have you ever noticed another person who seems so completely at peace with the world? They have given up their struggle and it seems as though they have transcended themselves; instead, they are experiencing the full joy of life. Maybe you recall a time when you experienced that level of happiness—feelings that stick with you and transcend both space and time—and you feel something more than just being alive. You can find that humor and joy in every day.

So, one final time: Are you an animal, a human, or both? Do you have what it takes to realize every aspect of your being, from the smallest pains and pleasures all the way to the creation of your own purpose and fulfillment?

Don't wait any longer to enjoy your life. *You are ready.* No one else can live it for you or tell you what to do. Life is worth the risk. Face your fears, remind yourself that you can do this, create a life that means something to you, and seek out others who need help. You only get one shot at this, as the person that you are now, so you can look at life and say, "Why bother?" or you can say, "Why not?"

Go out and *live* like you have nothing to lose!

Aut Viam Inveniam Aut Faciam

"I will either find a way or make one."

ACKNOWLEDGEMENTS

I'm extremely grateful to everyone in my life, but especially my friend Ben Grant. This book (like most good things in my life) would not be possible without the steady and unconditional support of a true friend. His feedback and encouragement were invaluable and kept me going throughout this process since this project began as a series of personal journal entries.

I'd also like to thank my editor Jessie Raymond for all her hard work. Apparently, ideas are my strong suit, not grammar and formatting. It was great to work with her.

And finally, I must acknowledge the best teacher of them all: Life. My experiences continue to teach me about how to live a good life in this world. Here's to keeping an open mind and learning as we go.

Matt Dellaero currently resides all over the world! Remote work is pretty cool.

Printed in the USA
CPSIA information can be obtained
at www.ICGtesting.com
LVHW021550261024
794703LV00016B/717